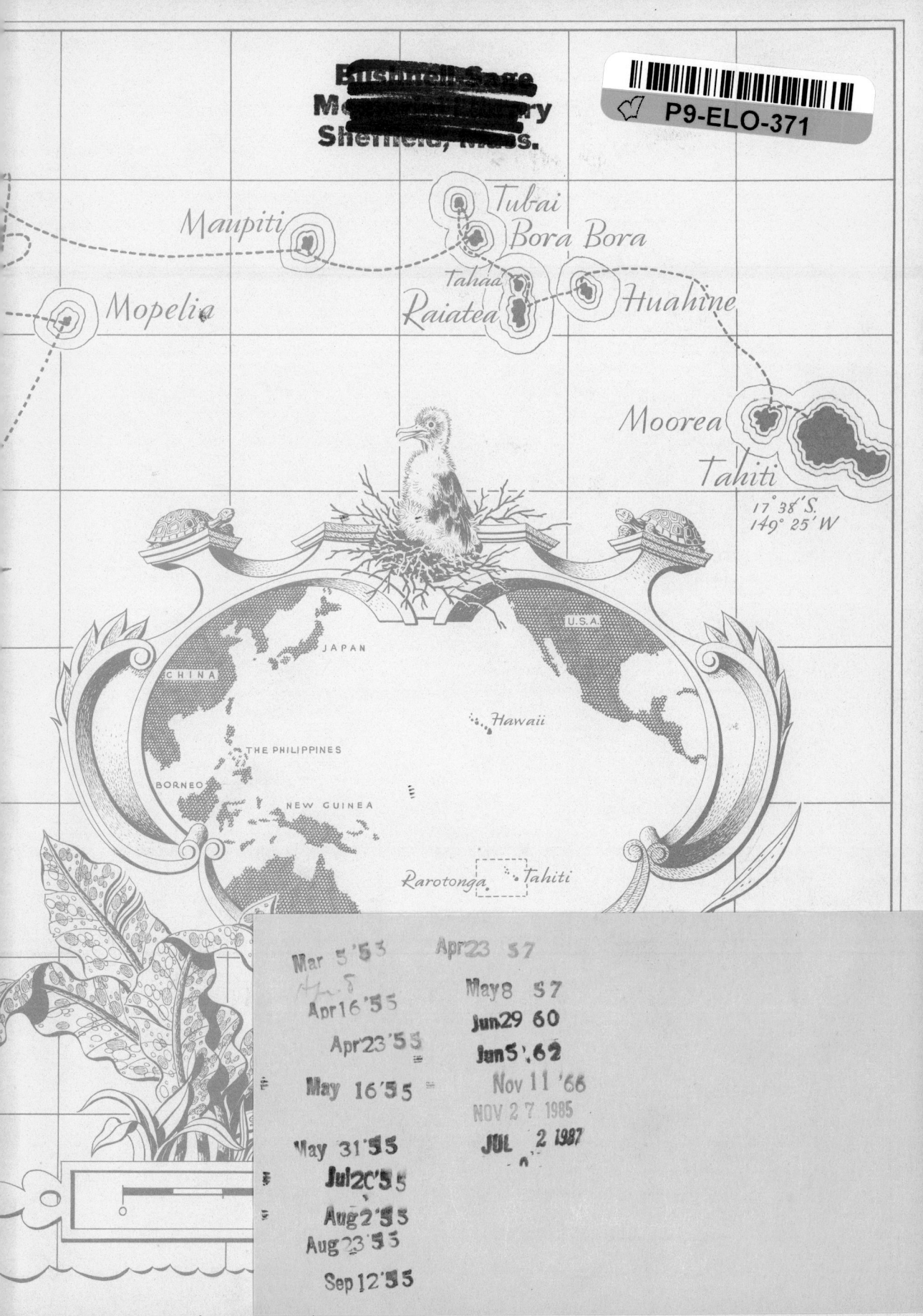

Maupiti

Tubai
Bora Bora

Mopelia

Tahaa
Raiatea

Huahine

Moorea
Tahiti

17° 38' S.
149° 25' W

JAPAN

U.S.A.

CHINA

Hawaii

THE PHILIPPINES

BORNEO

NEW GUINEA

Rarotonga   Tahiti

TAHITI

Voyage Through Paradise

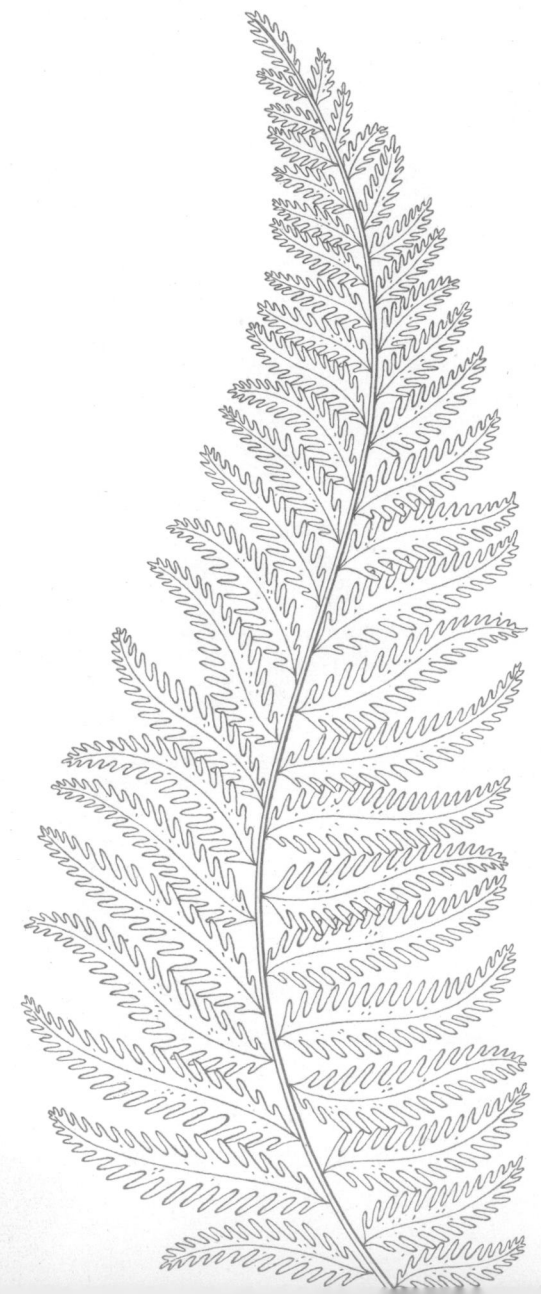

"Tahitians — God's best, at least God's sweetest works."
— *Robert Louis Stevenson*

TAHITI

Voyage Through Paradise

*The story of a small boat passage through
the Society Islands*

By
GEORGE T. EGGLESTON

With a photographic log by the author

THE DEVIN-ADAIR COMPANY · NEW YORK

A portion of TAHITI: Voyage Through Paradise
has been selected to appear in the October 1953
READER'S DIGEST *and its seventeen international*
editions, published in twelve languages.

———

TO HAZEL

Acknowledgments

WHEN ONE spends the better part of a year outside the country living the events narrated in this book many acknowledgments are in order. The author is, first of all, indebted to his mother who cared for our daughter, Day, while we were away. Without her tender indulgence the voyage could never have been attempted.

In Tahiti we were indebted to the James Norman Halls for their hospitality and encouragement. We thank Clayton Knight, an old friend of the Halls, for introducing us to them. For the many heart-warming contacts mentioned in the story we want to pay especial tribute to those noble people, the Tahitians who on all ten islands became our friends.

We are grateful to Harry Close for having been in Papeete with *Viator* at the precise moment we met him. We are also indebted to him for the interesting picture on page 215. To Dwight Long, thanks for the fine pictures on pages 178, 220, 222, and 231.

In the actual preparation of the book for press we are thankful for the publishing imagination of Devin Garrity and Thomas O'Conor Sloane III of the Devin-Adair Company. For the care and handling of the pictures and text for printing we thank Harry Wisner, Philip Kolb, Eustis Rawcliffe, James Dobyns, Ken Williams, Jr. and Anson Hosley of the Case-Hoyt Corporation.

PREFACE

A wonderful lot of stories have been written about the islands of the South Pacific. Long before the battles of the greatest war had made people conscious of names like the Marianas, The Gilberts, The Solomons, The New Hebrides, and the Fijis, my wife and I had gathered a shelf of South Pacific tales that touched upon islands of a vast triangle stretching from New Zealand to Hawaii to Peru. In our armchair travels we had come to know many magic place-names: the Australs, the Tuamotus, the Marquesas, Tonga, Samoa, Easter Island, and Pitcairn. And, as we read more and more, we learned that the unquestioned queen of all the islands was Tahiti, rising majestically over its immediate group, the Society Islands, and supra-supreme over all the ten thousand and one islands of the Pacific.

We read tributes to Tahiti and her sister isles by Bougainville, Darwin, and Captain Cook; by Herman Melville, Robert Louis Stevenson, and Jack London. Two hundred years ago, navigator Bougainville had said of Tahiti: "I thought I was walking in the Garden of Eden." Robert Louis Stevenson called the Tahitians "God's best—at least God's sweet-

est works." The late James Norman Hall spent most of his life writing of the wondrous charms of this particular group of islands, and died in the spot he loved above all others on this earth, Tahiti.

We guessed, thanks to our reading that we might find an idle yacht in Tahiti's port of Papeete and charter it for a leisurely dream cruise into the shallow lagoons and fabled bays of the outer islands of the Society group.

Our guess came true. Papeete was, is, and always will be a port of crewless yachts waiting for charters that never come. We are the only ones, so far as we know, who have discovered and acted upon this yachting phenomenon. As we did it, others can do the same.

G. T. E.

Hickory Bluff
Rowayton, Conn.

CONTENTS

TAHITI

Voyage Through Paradise

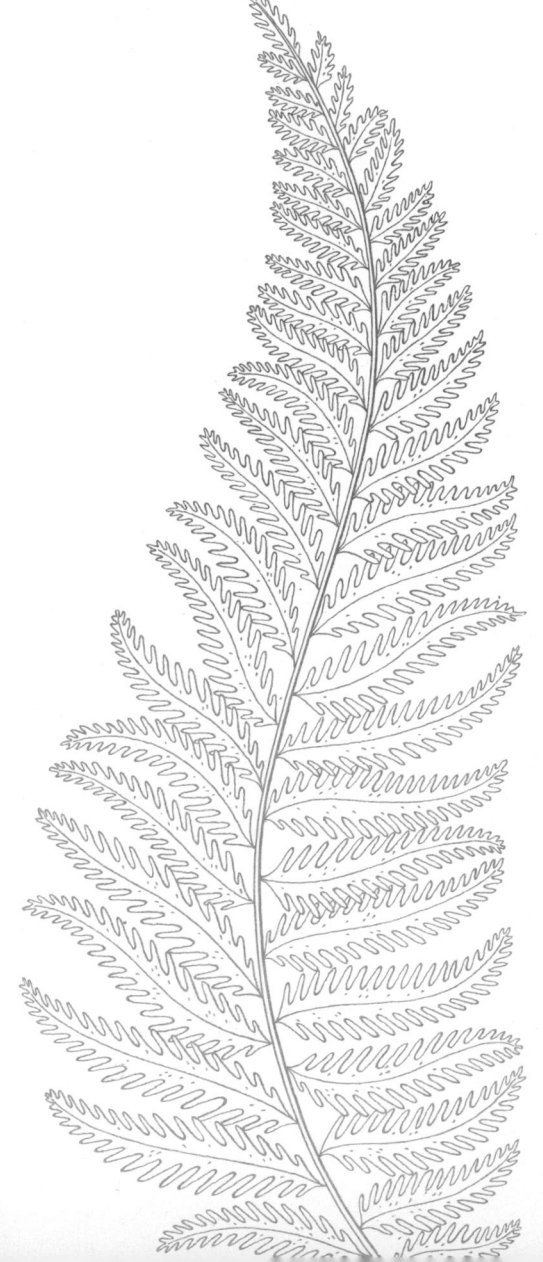

The First Island—TAHITI

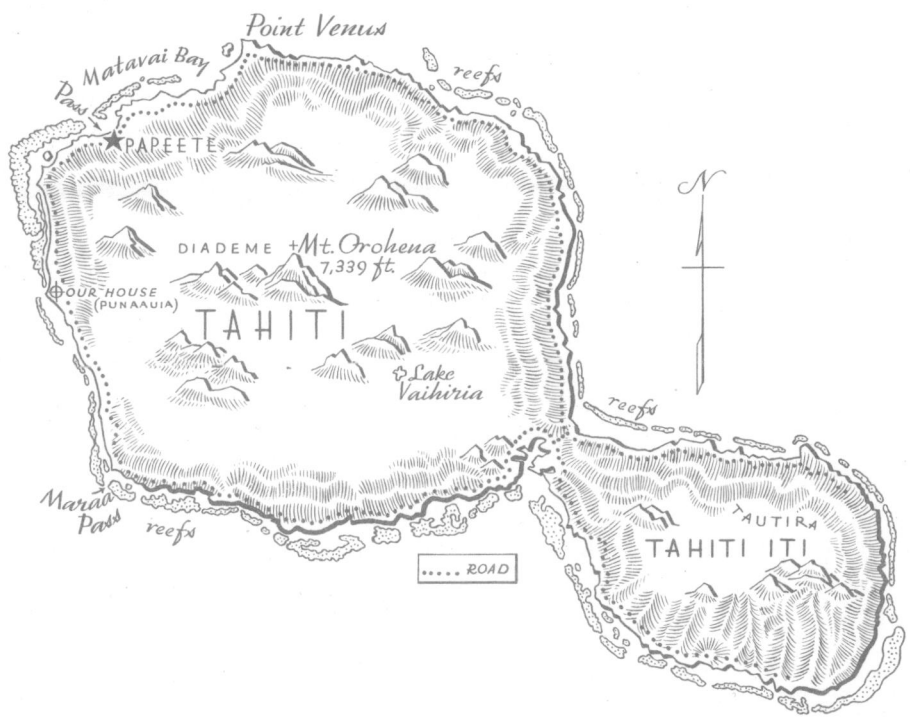

IT WAS a spring night, yet it held for us all the pleasant tensions of a night before Christmas. It had been fourteen days since we boarded the tiny French steamer at Panama to begin the long, slow crawl across the equatorial Pacific. The *Ville de Strasbourg*, en route from Marseille to New Caledonia with a semiannual supply of building materials and administrators for the Colonial possessions, had been our only means of getting to the Society Islands. She was to make one stop, Tahiti, before proceeding to the western Pacific.

The days at sea had been so quiet, the weather so calm, that a sailing canoe might have made the 4,493-mile traverse without taking a single dollup of water over the gunwales.

We gave up trying to sleep at about midnight. In our dressing robes, we climbed to the bridge of the vessel to gaze ahead into the moon and starlight. At 4:30 a.m. a vision appeared. We saw a great high mass of island, shrouded in misty moonglow. Soon the first rays of dawn dispersed the haze over our bows, and Tahiti lay before us, a bright chartreuse cutout on a staging of royal blue. Presently we saw purple-gray cloud masses encircling a series of mighty peaks as deep-creasing shadows appeared where volcanic valleys dropped to the sea. We rounded Point Venus light and the silhouette of the high mountain, Orohena; an hour later we were off the pass of the legendary capital of the Pacific, Papeete.*

As the *Ville* eased her rusty hulk along the ancient quayside, we looked past a forest of trading-schooner spars to the snug Quai du Commerce, acacia-shaded and drowsy in the heavy-scented morning air. Here and there a gleam of pastel-colored stucco picked up a bit of sunshine. A half dozen bicycles glided through the lights and shadows, while a bus full of outlanders came to a stop near the dock, unloading to the accompaniment of shrill laughter and the squeals of trussed pigs carried on the roof.

A very white sea bird glided to water level near us, its under plumage picking up the reflected pale green of the lagoon.

We had a considerable accumulation of gear to cart to the customs table, located in one end of a strong-smelling copra** storage shed. But the friendly customs officer didn't bother about anything except our phonograph records. These had to be "held for inspection," and were returned to us when we left the island. Our bags, full of cameras, photo supplies, charts, sextant, and chronometer, went through unopened and unchallenged. Later we were amused to reflect upon all the boxes of spare "things" we had carried over those thousands of miles of ocean. Local Chinese stores stocked every kind of sundry in abundance. We were to find American cigarettes, camera film tropically sealed, almost every brand of American toothpaste, flashlight bulbs, rubber bands, paper clips, typewriter ribbons, and even yo-yos.

From customs we proceeded, with the help of a young native porter, out along the seawall to a tired-looking structure across the road from the forest of masts we had seen. This, the Hotel Stuart, was the handiest stopping place available near the dockside. Mrs. Stuart, barefoot and smiling, met us at the door and showed us to our suite — a room and balcony overlooking the lagoon — at $1.50 per person per day, including Continental breakfast. The room was sparsely furnished, but very clean. Prominently displayed over the dresser was a notice to the effect that

Rhymes with Tahiti.

**Coconut meat.*

ladies of the evening were *persona non grata* with the management. Plainly, Mrs. Stuart ran a respectable place. This was further brought home to us when we asked for our key. No guest had ever requested one before, and our hostess was visibly hurt. The hotel simply had no keys, doors were rarely closed and never locked, and over the years there had thus far been no complaints.

We greatly enjoyed the several days we spent under Mrs. Stuart's hospitable tin roof. We first roamed the waterfront to see if any yachts were available needing crews. There were two — both too large — 70, 80 feet over-all, and therefore not the right things for getting into the shallow anchorages of the distant isles we had on our dream itinerary.

Next we did the typical tourist junket, a bicycle pilgrimage out the north shore road to Captain Cook's monument. This excursion was wonderful except for the bicycles. We made the mistake of renting rebuilt affairs instead of getting the new French or English equipment. Our bicycles were most carefully painted — black enamel with fancy gold hairlines all over them, but in the course of the trip they fell apart like trick circus bikes and we had to put the chains on so many times that we would have done better walking.

We went first to Taharaa Headland—old "One Tree Hill." Here, 500 feet above a crescent of black coral beach, we gazed upon the waters of Matavai Bay, where rested the *Dolphin* of Captain Samuel Wallis. He planted the British flag on June 24, 1767, and named the island George III in deference to his sovereign. Then eight months later came Bougainville. He planted the flag of France and named what he thought to be his discovery, Nouvelle Cythère, a title which also failed to supplant the name Tahiti in the history books. Here, too, Captain Cook's *Endeavor* dropped anchor on April 11, 1769. But the Great Navigator didn't tinker with the island's name, and he sailed on to chart Huahine, Raiatea, Tahaa, and the rest, calling the entire group the Society Islands, for his sponsors, The British Royal Society.

On the way back we stopped at the private cemetery of Tahiti's rulers, all named Pomare, where a pair of coconut trees spiraled up, trunks entwined. Regaining the outskirts of Papeete we pushed our bicycles up Signal Hill, just in time for a Moorea sunset. Close to the base of the signal tower, where watchmen hoist symbols to herald approaching steamers, stood an easel. Palm tops fringed the lower border of the daubed-in canvas, and blue sea filled the middle area. Moorea, which lies 8 miles due west of Tahiti, sat on the canvas horizon against a pale sky. The artist reclined on the ground smoking a cigarette — waiting for the sinking sun to silhouette the real island before feverishly translating what he saw to his prepared canvas. Seconds would count, for the sun sinks fast in the tropics. Brushes were ready and blobs of freshly squeezed yellows, reds and blues shimmered on the pallette. He caught something of what happened but some day an improved color-movie camera will seize the crashing fireworks of a Moorea sunset for the record. It is too fast-changing for the hand of man.

Long before sundown the French and English trading-company stores, the photography shops, the curio vendors, and the rest of the handful of white-owned enterprises of Papeete are shut and sealed. Five p.m. is their deadline and it is adhered to as religiously as the time-honored midday closing between 11:00 and 2:00. But the city continues to hum in the evening, even as it hums during the noon siesta. So numerous are the lighted Chinese shops, which cater to natives, that the few tightly shuttered occidental establishments are obscured in the blaze of activity.

Spider-webbing toward the hills from the Quai du Commerce are block on block of busy Chinese. They are Tahiti's mattress makers, cabinet makers, bicycle repairers, bakers, tailors, grocers, and hardware and dry-goods merchants, and they give service day and night. Their strangle hold on these businesses defies encroachment, and because they do work that no one else will do, their existence is pretty well justified. The natives have never made a pretense at being businessmen — even if they were, too many borrowing relatives would dissipate the profits — so they more than tolerate the bazaars operated by the penny-wise Chinese.

Only the French might legitimately begrudge the Chinese shopkeepers their foothold, but they do not because colonial shopkeeping is beneath their dignity. The French on the island confine their interests to the duties of officialdom or dabble in such things as copra and pearl-shell syndicates where sizeable fortunes are to be made. This is why there is no official anxiety to get tourist trade for the islands. This theory did not really impress itself upon us until we talked to some of the hotel-owning members of Papeete's Chamber of Commerce. They are up against perpetual friction in their efforts to get cruise ships and tourists to Tahiti. How they envy Hawaii, where the canners and sugar growers and hotel operators and cruise magnates have teamed up for years to keep the tourists coming. They pray that such a condition will come to pass on Tahiti and live in hopes that some day such an about-face will be possible.

Of course, the cruise-conscious merchants are wrong and when they have their way, Tahiti will have lost its charm. We admired the attitude of the antitourist faction and wished them well. At least they were making the native happy.

Little nontransferable plots of land furnish the islander with bread-fruit and coconuts, and the lagoons supply him with all the fish he needs. When he catches more than he can eat, he boards a bus and for a few centimes rides to Papeete, where he disposes of his surplus at the early-morning market and thus earns francs for the luxuries of the Chinese stores.

The buses, incidentally, are run purely for the benefit of the natives and they operate daily, bringing great human, animal, and vegetable cargoes in from the outlying districts. A ride on one is a never-to-be-forgotten experience and we had several. We counted 46 passengers on the bus that carried us and our bicycles from Punaauia one morning when we felt too tired to pedal the ten miles back to town.

We rode on the front seat with the driver, enjoying the traditional courtesy extended to newcomers, and under our feet was the driver's inevitable dog, chained to the steering post. Next to us sat a fat French-man, who held in his arms a portable radio, which he lifted into mid-air as we hit the worst chuck holes.

The two rear seats, we noticed, were piled with copra sacks and trussed pigs, forcing many of the passengers to sit in one another's laps. But the roof was really the astonishing thing. It had all of a dozen bicycles as well as copra, bananas, baskets of oranges, and papayas distributed fore and aft. Then, as if to hold all this down, a native in a broken armchair was enthroned in the middle. He set up a yell every time we rocked crazily around a turn; once, when we stopped, he poked his head into the bus and signaled one of the girls to come up and share his roost. One of them did, too, much to the amusement of the crowd.

In spite of the overcrowding, no one seemed put out. Children were breast-fed en route, and two guitars never missed a beat the entire trip. The bus, an American product, carried a small tin plaque on the dash which some Detroit engineer had carefully worded against just such a contingency. It said: "Notice: Overloading voids your warranty."

Were we disappointed in meeting the Tahitian head-on after all the things we had read about his race? Yes, and no. Tahiti, the melting pot where a century of intermarriage between native, white, and Chinese had left its confused aftermath, was really no place to find the answer. A few handsome examples of the Tahitians of legend were to be seen here and there upon the island. But only when we visited the distant isles did we see numbers of people more nearly like those described in a 1903 International Encyclopedia:

> Prepossessing, tall, symmetrically built. Handsome in form and feature. Sometimes excelling the ancient Greek in bodily vigor and statuesque beauty. With skin varying from brown to honey-tan, and features of European cast. Hair, dark, smooth and straight. In disposition naïve, sensitive, hospitable, courageous, sensual, happy, and eloquent in song and story.

Most ethnologists think that the progenitors of these people migrated from the Asiatic mainland in the first century A.D. They point to the fact that over the whole Polynesian area the languages show a common origin from one parent stock, the Malayan.

They write that these early peoples pushed out through the islands off the Indo-China coast in heavy war canoes, looking for a "Great Rising Sun Land" (Tawhiti-nui). As they went from island to island, finding the blacks of the far western Pacific too warlike and numerous to cope with, they gradually moved into the central South Pacific area, where the aborigines were notably docile. They are thought to have been in the Marquesas by the year 675, and Tahiti by 850. The 13th century was the great period of a secondary dispersal, with Tahiti the central point from which the new migrations took place. Around the year 1250 a group of Tahitian chiefs led a wave of expeditions to conquer Hawaii, 2,300 miles to the north. In the first half of the 14th century an armada of Tahitian war canoes left Rarotonga to descend 1,800 miles southward and take New Zealand from the aborigines.

That the present-day Tahitian is descended from a line of the most fearless navigators the world has ever known, is one point upon which all available data seem to be in agreement. Centuries before any European sailor had dared to venture outside the Straits of Gibraltar, Polynesian war canoes were ranging through all the islands within a 9,000-mile equilateral triangle cutting Hawaii on the north and New Zealand and Easter Island on the south. Some even sailed far south into the Antarctic Ocean, the legendary "cold sea beyond Rapa," to bring back tales of seals and icebergs.

How did these sea-borne nomads find their way around in that dim era, before such things as compass or sextant were known to man? The truth of the matter seems to be simply that they were natural sailors in complete mastery of the sea. They were so familiar with every navigational star in the sky that the heavens served them as a well-marked road map. They knew every slight slant and sound of the shifting trade winds. They knew where to look for cloud formations massing over isles below the horizon. They knew the currents and scend of the swells. They knew where homing birds were heading. They knew how to keep their hundred-foot double canoes afloat through any kind of weather. They knew when to lower their huge mat sails against a violent squall and when to run before a blow.

The heritage of this mighty race may still be seen in the natives of the present day. But gone are the days of the Greek gods—particularly around Papeete. Because of mixed intercourse, white man's diseases carried off whole generations of the best. Ravages of "civilization" were visited unto the children and grandchildren, and now the flashing white teeth that Captain Cook once saw are legend. Many of Tahiti's finest sons went away to World Wars I and II to die in France and on the Normandy beachheads.

One of the curious spots we visited in Papeete was the Yacht Club, where we went once or twice for cocktails. The club is mostly a spacious verandah, one rickety flight up from street level. It is a tradition that no resident member of the Tahiti Yacht Club owns a boat: visiting yachtsmen supply the boats, while the local club members supply the hospitality.

The small bar and billiard room were full of pictures of the late Zane Grey and various swordfish he landed during his angling career. Although permanently open doors were everywhere, Tahiti's Yacht Club had one more means of ventilation. A large aperture in the wall, caused by shellfire from a German warship in World War I, remains unmended; one can chat through it to the bartender beyond. The cruisers *Scharnhorst* and *Gneisenau* had come in to replenish their supplies in September 1914 and had been defied by a small French gunboat, the *Zéelée*. The Germans sank the *Zéelée* and dropped a few shells into the center of town, then fled and were later sunk off the Falkland Islands by Admiral Sturdee. The anniversary of the "bombardment" is celebrated as a holiday each year and the club has purposely, according to the steward, "preserved the hole intact."

On the club verandah old Tahiti hand, Lew Hirshon, told us of the rescue of three native lads found near starvation on the reef of Bellingshausen. The trio, aged nine, eleven, and fifteen, had never been off their native isle of Mangareva, far south in the Tuamotus. They had heard from their elders great tales of the *hohoa teata* (the pictures that are alive) and had stolen a 22-foot open sailboat, counting on navigating across the trade wind to Tahiti for a week end at the cinema palace. They missed Tahiti by almost 100 miles and were very near death when they piled up at Bellingshausen, 900 miles from home. They had taken only two dozen coconuts aboard at the start, and some days after the last had been eaten, the two older boys said that if they did not sight land in three more days they would eat their young companion. At this point the terrified little chap spied land birds and conned the craft to the spot where natives carried them ashore. A trading schooner brought them to a Tahiti hospital, and after three weeks of recuperation they were shipped back to Mangareva without having seen a movie. This, thought a French magistrate, was punishment enough.

As one invariably puts off looking up the friend of a friend when visiting in a strange land, we had from day to day postponed looking up the James Norman Halls. One of their New York friends had suggested we see them, and finally we sent a note, which Hall promptly answered. One of those pleasing, brief friendships ensued which contribute so much to one's memories of a place. "I usually work until three every day," he wrote, "but anytime you can come will be jake with me."

We bicycled out one afternoon around four, catching him as he was mowing the last swath of the front lawn. He ran the lawn mower under a banana tree and asked us to make ourselves comfortable while he washed up and looked for a few bottles of beer. The Hall cottage, with green tin roof and wide, open living room that ran half way across the front, stood on the high side of the road and faced the sea from a thick setting of native trees. There was nothing to indicate where the property began or ended, other than a path which crossed the road and led down to a little thatched house on the edge of the lagoon. This looked to us like the perfect retreat for writing.

Hall sensed what we were thinking when he returned.

"That's our summer house. It's cooler than this in the hot season, but somehow I never liked it as a place to work. Maybe because the phonograph is there. When I get playing my favorite records I don't know when to stop."

"How about radio?" I asked.

"Never have had one in the house."

"That's right—I recall a bit of Hall verse on the subject:

> *. . . news of highest consequence*
> *I miss; and feast of wit and flow of soul.*
> *I do not care. Mid-ocean solitudes*
> *Offer as of old, a recompense . . ."*

"Where did you see that?"

"On the boat coming out. In an *Atlantic Monthly*, I believe."

"Completely forgot I sent that off. Must have written it a year or so ago."

And so it went. Hall really was a person out of touch and happy because of it. He hiked, bicycled, and played his collection of Caruso records for amusement. He wrote and browsed in his 2500-volume library for intellectual lift.

He was getting along quite nicely without the blessings of contemporary journalism, too. Newspapers and magazines had been on the household taboo list for years because "they always are the same—full of age-old problems artfully presented to disturb a reader's peace of mind."

It was hard to believe that this mild, soft-spoken man had once sought and lived through a series of adventures so dangerous that the odds against his ever coming out alive were perhaps a million to one.

Hall had been in England when war came in the summer of 1914. He had just concluded a bicycle trip through the English countryside, reveling in the atmosphere of long-dead British poets. He too wanted to write beautiful verse and indeed had dreamed of little else since his boyhood in Iowa. Yet, underneath this quiet ambition was a heart beating fiercely to put the world aright as he saw it. He joined the first queue of English recruitments he chanced upon, and went to France as a machine gunner with the 9th Royal Fusiliers. Hall participated in several months of the bloodiest trench warfare of the conflict, and through a miracle came out of it to fly for the Escadrille Lafayette and later for the A.E.F. In those little open-cockpit fighter planes of cloth and wire, *pilote de chasse* Hall shot down five Germans, was himself shot down twice, and came out at the Armistice with every decoration the French had to offer.

Quite naturally the conversation drifted around to some of the illustrious names one has ever associated with these Polynesian islands. It was in a lush valley of waterfalls not far from the house of Hall that a young Charles Darwin gazed in awe upon "a mountain gorge far more magnificent than anything I had ever before beheld." In another nearby valley a middle-aged Gauguin described his surroundings as "an immense palace, decorated by nature herself—hence these fabulous colors and this fiery but softened air." On board the *Resolution* at anchor a short hike from where we sat, the great Cook marked the year 1777 with the lines: "There is scarcely a spot on the universe that affords a more luxurious prospect."...

High in Hall's affections was Rupert Brooke, whose *Collected Poems* had long been an inspiration to him. Brooke had arrived in Tahiti early in 1914, and in Papara, 30 miles south of Papeete, the youthful poet had written *The Great Lover,* a special Hall favorite. Rupert Brooke was killed in action in France in 1915.

Another literary immortal, Pierre Loti, came to Tahiti to escape "modern sham, false luxury, uniformity, and imbeciles." Here in 1880 the classic *Le Mariage de Loti* was composed by the young ex-naval officer.

Herman Melville was most responsible for bringing James Norman Hall to these islands. As an Iowa lad of ten, Hall had read *Typee* in wide-eyed wonder and resolved upon reaching, some day, somehow, the South Seas.

Hall had an aversion to spending much time in Papeete. This he shared with both Robert Louis Stevenson and Jack London, who had found the port a far too seductive influence on their restless crews. London had sailed his 55-foot ketch-rigged *Snark* westward to the Solomons to sing evermore of the beauty of the Society Islands and their people. Stevenson moved his schooner *Casco* to Tautira, as far as one can go from Papeete and still be on Tahiti. Ashore he wrote:

> ... *here was I at last;*
> *Here found all I had forecast.*

Stevenson loved Tahiti so passionately he planned to spend the rest of his life there. He finally chose Apia, in Samoa, because his literary marts required access to the mail-packet lanes.

Sarah Hall was a charming and attractive woman. Her main interests were her home, her son Conrad, and daughter Nancy. She had a quiet sense of humor that on occasion could baffle the more inquisitive of the traveling literary people who called at the Hall home for material.

"Did you enjoy your husband's *Pitcairn's Island* as much as *Mutiny on The Bounty?*" one round-the-world author asked of Mrs. Hall.

"I don't know. I haven't read either one," she answered, with a sly wink at her husband.

Hall spoke affectionately of the other half of the writing team, his long-time friend Charles Nordhoff. (After the completion of the *Bounty* trilogy, there were destined to be no further important collaborations of the team. "Nordy" died in Tahiti in 1947, James Hall in 1951.)

The Halls' delightful spot "out in the country" a few miles north of Papeete made us yearn to spend a few weeks out of town ourselves. "Out in the country" on Tahiti is not the same proposition as out in the country most other places. The "country" on Tahiti means out along the beach in either direction from town.

The island of Tahiti is best described as two ranges of high mountains connected by a low isthmus. The total land area of some 400 square miles is comprised mainly of an uninhabited and trackless interior—a region of jagged peaks and very deep gorges from which scores of streams tumble down to the sea. A dense tropical vegetation covers everything except the steepest crags and cliffs. Only the hardiest of souls have ever attempted to trek into the interior, and Mount Orohena, highest island peak in the South Pacific, has defied the conquest of mountaineers since the beginning of time. Hall and a party of climbers once approached to within half a mile of the 7,300-foot summit, only to find that the crumbling volcanic rock and loose lava dust could not be mastered without bringing in some specially designed machinery.

Papeete, the island's only town, is rather bluntly described in the *U. S. Pilot Book:* "Seat of government of the Society Islands; sanitary conditions good; no endemic tropical fevers; tuberculosis common; elephantiasis prevalent; venereal disease rife and some leprosy." So we assumed the "country" would have its virtues.

The "country," or flat beach land, runs ninety miles around the base of the island proper, much the way the brim of a ten-gallon hat encircles the crown. A hundred yards out of town in either direction, coconut trees, thatched huts, and outrigger canoes are the keynote. One may travel around the island on the sole "highway," the famed Broom Road of Herman Melville, and all is pretty much the same. The island population numbers approximately 25,000, about half being concentrated in Papeete, the other half scattered around the shore line. From Papeete to Papeete, the impression is all thatch and outrigger. Wealthy Americans, perhaps half a dozen, maintain "villas" along the shore, but not one of these is out of key or pretentious. No touch of Hollywood has crept in anywhere.

On a stretch of white-sand beach at the lagoon's edge, ten miles south of town, we found just the place we wanted. It was in the Punaauia district, the country home of one of Papeete's official families.

We had made some preliminary inquiries in town about the place, but when we chugged up to the door in a borrowed flivver we were unprepared for the reception accorded us. Our prospective landlady and a couple of native girls were already on the scene. They had draped the place with garlands of freshly-cut hibiscus and *tiare* blooms, and on a bright red-and-white dining table cover of *pareu** cloth they had piled oranges, avocadoes, and papayas in a breathtaking arrangement.

"Ah, greetings, friends. Meet my nieces Mvana and Tina. We came out to have things ready in case you like it here. It is not different from many other places, but we have loved it. Perhaps, if you drive on out the road and look further, you will return to take this."

We reminded her that we expected to stay only a few weeks.

"You may stay six days or six months, it is all the same. There is only one rule—you must truly like it here."

**Pah-ray-oo.*

The three pandanus-and-bamboo bungalows on coconut-trunk stilts contained an inventory of everything we could possibly need. One bungalow contained a living room and dining room, another the sleeping quarters. The third was a cook house, and to it was attached, of all things, a shower and bath—supplied with unlimited icy water piped from a rocky basin far up the mountainside. True to form, our houses had no doors nor windows. Side walls were open all around and we could look upon the blue sea before us or the green foot-hills behind. Bamboo blinds and woven pandanus shutters could be lowered against the rains. But this was Tahiti's winter, and rains were rare. Coconut palms graced our immediate view in all directions, and bunches of ripe bananas hung from banana palms a few steps from the verandah.

We shared our hostess' enthusiasm for the place, and to look further was out of the question. She seemed to sense our appreciation of its beauty and was almost apologetic that the rent was $10.00 per week. As if to make up for charging us any rent at all, she showered kindnesses upon us. Even an outrigger canoe was presented for our use. Finally she threw a native-prepared feast for us at her daughter's home and proudly invited her entire family to shake our hands.

The great reef upon which the blue Pacific incessantly thundered and boomed was about a quarter of a mile out from the shore line. Beyond the reef, across a dozen miles of sea, lay the jagged profile of the island of Moorea, over which the sun obligingly set for us each evening in a display of pyrotechnics. The lagoon was a pool of inexhaustible wonders, and it tempted us into its cool depths a hundred times a day. With water goggles we explored the labyrinths of coral, ever calling to each other to share a newly found underwater vista of fantastic color. On the reef itself, when the surf was down, one could walk upon a strand of coral broad enough to embrace a four-lane highway. In the pools of its pitted surface, we found trapped fish and crawling shell forms that intrigued us by the hour.

Viewed from the reef, our tiny thatched bungalows seemed the only signs of life for miles in each direction. As far as the eye could see, palm fronds waved. The light green of the lagoon water, against the coral sand, formed the lower rim of an immense picture topped by the green peaks of the island, which swept upward through valley mists and chalk-white cloud shapes.

[27]

One day Hazel and I put our camera equipment into pressed-tin containers and paddled our outrigger toward the reef with an idea of getting some pictures of our surroundings from the sea. This was before we had learned to appreciate the whimsicalities of the surf. Just as we approached the reef's inner edge, an unusually heavy roller broke across the barrier from the outside and swept white and foaming toward us. Much of its energy was spent by the time it tumbled over into the lagoon, but in spite of all we could do, it threw the outrigger high and flipped us into the water, scattering our gear in every direction. The scene must have resembled the famed one described in *Moby Dick*, where the whale boat shoots into the air and the crew summersaults hither and yon.

The danger for us was that we might be rolled against coral heads and badly cut or bruised. Luckily we suffered only a few bad scratches on our legs. The tinned camera gear floated, and after fifteen minutes of swimming around we had righted the canoe, baled it out, and gathered things together for a retreat homeward.

Oddly enough, the scratch of the inanimate coral is the thing most feared in these islands. No quadrupeds roam the hills or valleys, other than a few harmless pigs and cattle. There are no snakes, leopards, poisonous spiders, alligators, or any other of the living things most often thought of as thriving in the tropics.

Sharks are the most widely heralded villains, yet sharks of any size rarely come into the lagoon shallows. We were to see many during our voyaging, but none more than five feet long in a lagoon. These small fry always seemed as afraid of us as we were of them.

There are, however, three denizens of the lagoons that are of the stuff of which nightmares are made. They are rare enough, though, to be far outranked as menaces by the coral itself. One is the moray eel, which has been reported to uncoil its ten-foot length from a reef crevice and fasten vicelike fangs into the arm of an unwary diver. Another is the octopus, sometimes as much as fourteen feet between tentacle tips, also living in deep coral. The third is the *nohu*, a bottom fish with barbs on its back. The *nohu* lurks just under the sand, ready to inject rattle-snake-like poison into any unshod foot that comes into contact with it. We kept away from the depths just inside the reef to avoid the first two, and always wore sneakers as armor against the *nohu*.

Our coral scratches required special treatment. South Sea coral cuts, even tiny ones, can, if neglected, take years to heal. A black salve had been recommended to us in Papeete. The salve keeps the cut open, allows the coral poison to drain out, and starts the healing from the bottom up rather than from the top down. We were warned to keep out of the lagoon waters while the cuts were healing, and so for the better part of a week we explored the foothills.

We poked around the ruins of an old French fort, perched about 1,000 feet up the hillside, commanding the narrow entrance to Punaauia valley. Looking down from the crumbling ramparts we tried in vain to spot our bungalows. So thick was the carpet of waving palm fronds on the island's rim that no sign of habitation was visible anywhere.

One day, from nowhere, Timi I appeared. He beached his outrigger on our place, and by way of introduction presented us with a dozen freshly speared fish. Timi (Tahitian for Jimmy) was the first of a series of Timis who turned up during our voyage. Like the others, he proved thoroughly lovable but rather unpredictable. His English vocabulary was limited, but we soon found there was nothing he wanted from us but some pictures of himself.

Timi I was a good-looking fellow—in his late twenties and strong as an ox. He could run up a coconut tree as fast as a ten-year-old and was marvelous in the heavy brush with a machete. He had a wife and children somewhere down the beach; we never saw them, but we gathered they hardly missed him in his wanderings.

Timi had an odd sense of humor and sometimes it was hard to tell when he was joking and when serious.

We asked him if he could lead us to the old burial caves which we had heard were on a series of ledges above the fort. He looked shocked.

"*Tabu Tabu.*"

"You mean nobody goes there?"

"No good."

"You take us there tomorrow?"

"No good."

"Take us there tomorrow and we will take pictures."

"Sure," and he grinned broadly.

Late the following afternoon Timi appeared with an extra-large machete and a coal-oil lantern.

"Follow me," said Timi, and armed with sandwiches and camera we set off. For about an hour we slogged through a dark bog created by a particularly dense grove of coconut. At length we came on a deserted hut at the base of a heavily wooded cliff. Here Timi tested the edge of his machete blade, looked up into the dense growth ahead, and frowned.

"*Tabu.* No good," he said. Then he pointed to the camera and grinned. "Okay?"

So, as he commenced to chop his way, singing, into the tangle of vines, we took pictures of him and his machete in action. The heat under the dense growth was damp and oppressive, and we were perspiring like steambathers when at last we came upon an old disused trail that led up to some great outjuttings of volcanic rock. Once we were among the rock formations, our curiosity was satisfied. Tucked into the many crevices were grinning skulls and disintegrating bones. This was apparently a burial ground that hadn't been used or visited for years. The caves did not go in very deep, but were so arranged as to be perfectly protected from the weather.

Timi proved to be a great deal busier crawling around among the remains of his ancestors than we had expected. He was particularly proud of the evidences of good teeth everywhere, and insisted on posing with a perfect specimen of jaw bone.

"Good—good," he remarked, as he carefully replaced it in the niche where it belonged.

We had been curious about the lantern which Timi had brought along, but soon we learned that it was not without reason. Timi, a most forehanded individual, had planned a totally unexpected itinerary for us, once we had done with the burial caves. Instead of returning by way of the route we had come, Timi led us around the cliff wall and down into an abrupt valley, through which ran a tiny stream. The whole valley might best be described as a gigantic rock garden; the stream cascaded from rocky pool to pool as though it had been planned by some master landscape gardener.

Darkness overtook us here, and Timi sprang his real surprise. He produced two small, six-pronged spearheads which he had been carrying in his hat band, cut a pair of five-foot sticks to which he attached the barbs, turned up the lantern to its highest candlepower, and motioned us to follow as he stepped suddenly to the edge of a very still pool. Quickly passing the lantern to us, he darted his spear into the water and out again—in and out, in and out, with such speed that we were at a loss to know what in the world he was attempting to do. After a couple of minutes of these lightning endeavors he paused, turned to us with a grin, and held out a handful of the famed Tahitian fresh-water shrimp. It was unbelievable — shrimp from a tropical mountain stream.

We were so entranced by the nocturnal shrimp-spearing that we spent hours following the stream down to the road home. After a few hundred near misses of the tiny targets, we too became fairly proficient in the spearing art. The trick was to approach a pool as quietly as possible and expose its clear depths suddenly to the light. At this point, all is motionless and to the uninitiated there is nothing in the water but a few old leaves. But the practiced eye will take in the whole pool at a split second's glance and note the pairs of small red eyes brightly reflected under a leaf here, under a rock there. The instantaneous survey is all-important; one must spear swiftly, from memory, for at this precise moment all hell breaks loose in the shrimp world.

Quicker than trout they flick about madly in all directions; some even land obligingly at one's feet on the rocks. They never stop moving until the spear hits them, and to the amateur it seems at first absolutely impossible to connect with them. The shrimp have all the agility of fleas plus the stamina of Columbia River salmon. Between us we gathered the equivalent of a bucketful and carried our catch home in a basket Timi plaited of palm leaves for the occasion. They averaged three to four inches in length and were delicious eating—raw for Timi, cooked for us.

Our burial-cave-and-shrimping expedition was the only up-country trekking we attempted before leaving the island. The next time we visit Tahiti we will schedule a hike inland to the island's little-known Lake Vaihiria, high in the interior and surrounded by tremendous peaks, "where only the spirits dwell." This, the single mountain lake in all the islands of French Oceania, requires a day-and-a-half climb to gain its 1,400-foot elevation. According to legend, lizard men who are today reincarnated in the form of monster eels inhabit the lake's black depths.

A dozen or so miles south along our road we visited the water grotto at Maraa. Here, a few steps inland, one looks upon a rippled pool within a fairyland cavern. From its sides and dome hang ferns which drip rain upon the surface below. The pool looks short enough for one to throw a pebble along its length with ease. But so far this feat has never been performed. We were told that the "Tupapau" of Maraa downs every stone in midflight.

Opposite the grotto, lagoon waters add to the fantasy of the area by spouting forth a number of fresh-water springs; these burble up through the sand and brine of the shallows like miniature fountains.

The road from our bungalow to Maraa and back was a gaudy stretch. The way was studded with small flowering trees which bore exotic names; maid of Moorea, queen of night, frangipani, *tiare Tahiti*. The cream-and-amber blooms of the frangipani half hide the whiter-than-snow *tiare*. Bushes of crimson hibiscus, accented by scattered royal poinciana, shared their places in the sun with mango, orange, lime, guava, and purple bursts of bougainvillea.

This bit of road, this horticulturist's dream, is no product of civic planning—it may be encountered here, there, and everywhere about the island.

Our weeks in the country were not all devoted to canoeing and hiking. We spent long afternoons rereading books about the islands, studying up on our navigation and going over the charts which we had brought along from New York. The more we read and talked things over, the more we became fixed upon the idea that, rather than attempt to see too much, we would try to concentrate our islands within the approximately 1,000-mile radius between the easternmost of the Society group and the southernmost of the Cook Islands.

The more we read the more convinced we became that we would find just the craft we wanted for the voyage. Papeete, as a port of call for yachts, had a consistently sad record. Book after book related how such and such small yacht, bound west around the world, had put in at Papeete only to be stuck there for months on end because the crew jumped ship to woo the pretty girls. Many a bedeviled skipper abandoned his cruise altogether, and eventually got a new crew and returned to the States Some boats were abandoned by both crew and owner and left for sale to the highest bidder. Papeete was in truth a port of broken cruises.

Certainly the story of the *Bounty* mutiny was not the last
for Tahiti's harbor. Just as Captain Bligh's men had put him
returned to the lures of the island's 18th-century belles, so h
line of American yachts suffered from the same disrupting
Here was the reason for the idle masts across from the Hotel

The morning we closed up our little houses and headed fc
an old car Timi had negotiated for us, we were full of high h
conversation. We had a feeling that any day now we would
boat for us in the harbor. We bounced along over the ruts an
the old Broom Road and reminisced about the sailing we h
at home. Our cruising there had been limited to the waters
New York and Nantucket Sound, and we felt most proficien
typical, overnight cruising boat of about 30 feet. We knew th
into the islands where only small passes gave entry to lagoon
ages, we would have to find something about this over-all len{

Our friends on the yacht club verandahs at home had ma
nous predictions about our plans. When we left New York,
were running that we would be back on an early, Americ*
freighter. Comfortably housed suburban couples, they said, ju
pick up and go small-boat sailing in the South Seas.... This
sailing might be high adventure for a pair of college boys, bu
desk-bound commuter and his garden-clubbing wife, island-h
in such cramped quarters would be terribly uncomfortable if not
right dangerous.

As if by magic, we were suddenly confronted with exactly t
of boat we had been talking about.

I had pulled the car to a stop before the Stuart, and for five n
the two of us just sat and stared. Stern to the sea wall was th
white hull of a tiny schooner — a newcomer in the harbor. W
started to speak at once. Her name and hailing port: *Viato*
Francisco.

It's a wonder we managed to get our bags out of the car and in
Stuart. For the next couple of hours the *Viator* (traveler) was the
of all things for us. Her owner was Harry Close, a bronzed young o
going skipper who had sailed her out of the Golden Gate some m
before and proceeded to Tahiti via Hawaii, the Marquesas, an
Tuamotus. He had started with a crew of three young yachtsmen

had signed on in great enthusiasm and lost interest along the way. He made a change of personnel in Honolulu and signed on a native lad in the Marquesas; now, in Papeete, his *Viator* was as crewless as so many others had been in exactly the same place.

Close had picked up a lot of yarns about the other boats in the harbor, which had all experienced some form of trouble. George Vanderbilt, whose palatial *Cressida* was tied up nearby, had had one of the oddest stories to tell. He had come aboard the *Viator* that very morning and jokingly offered to swap his 172-foot schooner outright for Harry's little pumpkin seed. His crew had taken to crawling into the *Cressida's* refrigerator compartments and developing cases of acute frostbite so they could be hospitalized in Papeete and left behind to enjoy the island's charms unhampered by working. Under Admiralty law, Vanderbilt was obliged to leave funds behind to pay the crew's bills, as well as steamer fares back to the United States. Acute frostbite was a malady so unusual in these latitudes that the local medical fraternity was in quite a quandary as to how to treat it.

The *Big Dipper*, a 70-footer which had been chartered in Boston by a scientific expedition, also had arrived with a hull full of troubles during our sojourn out on the beach. She had weathered a hurricane in the Caribbean and had come through the Canal for a leisurely stop of several weeks in and around the Galapagos; thence to Tahiti, taking, in all, seven months since her departure from Boston. Just nine days out of Papeete she started to leak like a sieve and everyone had to man the pumps to keep her afloat until they could get her on the ways of the local boat yard. Her hull was badly shot through with dry rot, and all aboard her shuddered, while at the same time marveling that she had come so far afloat. The owner was having her fixed, but the crew used all that had happened as an excuse to jump ship and drink deep of the island's pleasures. Not the least of the *Dipper's* troubles was that sloshing bilge water had taken the labels off several hundred cans of supplies, so that every time the cook wanted a can of beef he had to open twenty-five cans of blackberry jam, or whatever, to find it. The annoyed cook tossed overboard enough mistakenly opened canned goods to stock a small grocery store.

We hit it off with Harry right from the start. He said he planned to sail back to the States eventually, but was eager to poke around the

outer islands we had marked out on our charts, and if we felt the three of us could get along, he did. We could cruise through a thousand miles of islands with him and eventually get to the steamer lane, and catch a freighter home. He would have as good a chance of recruiting a crew later on as now.

The Winslow-designed *Viator* was exactly 32 feet over-all. Being about lifeboat size, she had to be a marvel of compactness below to get in her four bunks, galley, and enclosed head, and still carry enough gear for months at sea. We three had done enough sailing to know how not to get in each other's hair on a small boat. Many of our charts fitted in, our sextant and chronometer were welcome additions to double check those on board, and that Hazel and I had a bond of common interests with Harry was apparent when we found that the *Viator's* selection of books coincided in many respects with our own.

For the next few days we were busy packing all our extra stuff for shipment home. The things we took aboard *Viator* were but a fraction of the contents of the trunks and bags we had landed on Tahiti. It is amazing what one can get along without when the going really calls for traveling light.

Carrying supplies aboard *Viator* or any other vessel at Papeete's quayside is vastly simplified by the unusual behavior of the tides in this area. The rise and fall is so negligible (8-10 inches) that permanent gangplanks extend from sea wall to boats along the entire waterfront. Tahiti is the only place in the world where tides ignore the effect of the moon and follow the sun. With lows at 6 a.m. and 6 p.m. each day; highs at noon and midnight, it is not too difficult to tell the time by watching the water mark on the sea wall.

We hated to say goodbye to William Crake. Many others had been hospitable, but Crake was the guardian of our film, and his like would not be found again in our cruise west. We had grown accustomed to his "Ah, well, I think I can have prints for you by Monday." His get-up, too, struck our fancy. His main attire was a red-flowered *pareu* worn around the loins. A pair of Mary-Jane canvas pumps, as white as his hothouse skin, always graced his small feet. His scholarly face was pince-nezed, and a dead cigarette habitually hung on his lower lip. Aside from tending his canaries on the verandah or calling an order into the kitchen, where his large black native woman and children held forth, he was at your service to talk photography. And he knew plenty about the subject.

In the years since 1911, when he forsook Australia for the islands, Crake had served a steady stream of amateur photographers. J. P. Morgan, Vanderbilt, Astor, Crocker, and Allan Villiers had all taken their business to him. It was he who warned us most graphically on film care. Ninety per cent of the film that came to him for processing had already been spoiled by exposure to humidity.

Yet in all his years of photography, William Crake had made few pictures. He had been too preoccupied for "even a self-portrait," and when we made a shot of him he requested leave to print a batch of copies for relatives in New Zealand. In looking at the finished article he said, "Ah, well, I haven't deteriorated as much as I thought."

Louis Bernicot was the last Tahiti acquaintance we made. He had sailed his 41-foot sloop *Anahita* from Bordeaux to Papeete, via the Straits of Magellan, and what's more, did it single-handed. When he set foot ashore at Bordeaux again, he would share honors with Captain Slocum, the only lone circumnavigator of the globe (via the Straits of Magellan) so far on the books. His boat was a marvel of arrangement. Although most of the time he had lashed the tiller and let her sail herself, averaging 90 miles a day on jib alone in gales of the deep South Pacific, there was an enclosed wheelhouse complete with bunk, where he could relax close to the compass during long periods of wet, tricky weather. The cabin below was quite roomy and exceptionally comfortable for reading and working navigation problems. The galley was conveniently located under the fore hatch, through which he could scramble, when necessary, to douse the jib or operate roller-reefing gear at mealtime.

Bernicot's voyage was the realization of an ambition of long standing. Years before, while managing the French Line office in Galveston, Texas, he had resolved someday to retire and sail around the world alone. At anchor in Tahiti, he had much of the worst behind him. Having no crew, and therefore no crew troubles, the only hurdles ahead were wind and water. We wished him *bon voyage* with all our hearts.

The afternoon *Viator* weighed anchor for Moorea was, in the language of yacht-club sailors at home, "a hand-picked day for sailing." The little group of friends who were down to see us off waved some last-minute advice, a policeman tossed us a bag of mail marked "Rarotonga, direct," and we slipped our moorings with a short sail ahead to our first anchorage. Once well out in the harbor, past Motuiti (little island), the vessel seemed to answer to the clap of wind in her sails by fairly leaping ahead. As we went through the pass into the purple sea beyond, we all shared that small-boy thrill that comes to one so rarely after childhood. We drove through the lines of short, steep rollers outside the reef, and our craft seemed to take on a businesslike attitude as she settled down to footing her way across the famous channel. In spite of the whipping of the halliards and the steady rush of wind through the rigging, an atmosphere of profound peace had possession of the boat. Our offshore cruising at home had never brought quite the same thing. We were to learn that only South Pacific ocean depths below a small hull can produce the effect. Hazel took the tiller while Harry and I put on the fisherman staysail. The few extra yards of canvas boosted our speed a fraction of a knot or so. Now a half dozen porpoises were squiring us along, describing their half-submerged arcs in slow motion yet somehow keeping abreast of our slicing bow. We looked on Tahiti for the last time, the green peaks from our sea-level view seeming twice as high as they had from the steamer deck so many weeks before.

The Second Island—MOOREA

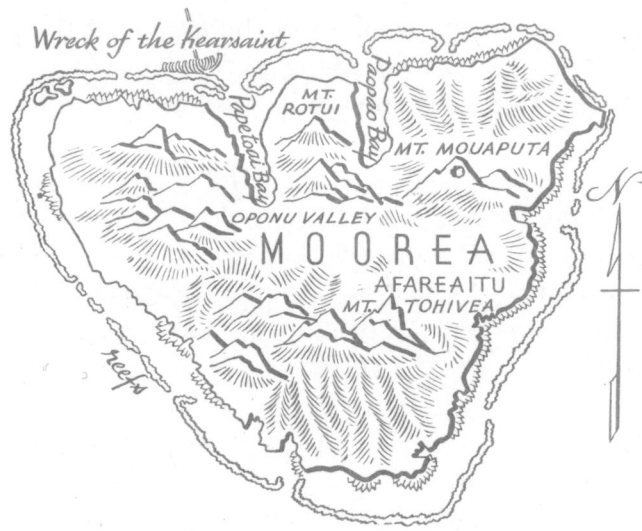

SEEN from Tahiti, Moorea had always been a purple shape on a backdrop of sea and sky. Now it was emerging in its true colors. If anything, it seemed greener than its sister island. It was certainly more rugged. It rose out of the sea with Gibraltarlike abruptness, and its peaks outsawtoothed the Sierra Nevadas.

In an hour and a half the spanking breeze had put us around the northeast tip of the island; we relaxed in the certainty of making our anchorage well before dusk. As we glided closer to the reef-tossed surf, we were able to pick out landmarks from the charts which indicated that Papetoai Bay was not more than another hour's sail ahead. The *Pilot Book* told us more:

> The island is almost an equilateral triangle in shape, each side being 8 miles in length, and the northern side taking about an east and west direction; it is surrounded by a barrier reef through which are several passes to the basins between it and the shore. On the northern side are two deep harbors named Papetoai and Paopao Bays, which afford snug and safe anchorages. These two are scarcely two miles apart, but between them rises Mt. Rotui, with several peaks, the highest of which is 2,884 feet.
> *Papetoai Bay. Directions:*—The wreck of the French Cruiser Kearsaint, on the west side of the entrance, is a good navigational mark for entering but should be given a berth of not less than 200 yds.

Once past Paopao Bay and Mount Rotui, we found an extra-blue gap in the reef, took down the fisherman, and headed abruptly toward the pass. To give the rusted remains of the *Kearsaint* the proper berth, we had to hug closely the breaking surf on our port hand; Harry climbed to the masthead and our pulses quickened to the sensation of coral piloting.

In spite of Moorea's position as the only land within sight of Tahiti, it is an isolated and forgotten island. It is hard to realize that less than a century ago, as one of the seats of residence of Tahiti's royal Pomares, it boasted a flourishing population and maintained a busy sailing-canoe intercourse with the larger island. In those days, foreign shipping called frequently at Moorea—mainly to engage in the court intrigues which were so much a part of the early struggles for trade advantage. After the fall of the Pomares, Moorea declined in importance, even to the French; today, it is just part of a Tahiti sunset—nothing more. A small semiweekly launch runs over from Papeete with supplies; a French official is in residence at Afareaitu on the east coast, but aside from his family and a handful of natives and whites, it is a deserted isle.

What a rare experience it must have been to saunter into the royal enclosure, as Melville did in 1843, and steal a peek at the Moorea palace of Queen Pomare IV. In *Omoo*, the sequel volume to *Typee*, Melville manages to strike up an acquaintance with a pretty little lady-in-waiting, who takes him into the 150-foot-long pandanus-thatched throne room of her majesty. He is quickly shooed out by the queen, but not before he has noted everything in great detail:

> The queen was a barefoot, matronly-looking woman dressed in a loose gown of blue silk, with two rich shawls, one of red and one of yellow, tied about her neck. Her features were not too handsome. Her facial expression was care-worn, her mouth voluptuous. She seemed about forty; but she is not so old.
> The whole scene was a strange one; but most surprising was the incongruous assemblage of the most costly objects from all quarters of the globe. Cheek by jowl they lay beside the rudest native articles, without the slightest attempt at order. Superb writing-desks of rose-wood, inlaid with silver and mother-of-pearl; decanters and goblets of cut glass; embossed volumes of plates; gilded candelabras; sets of globes and mathematical instruments; the finest porcelain; richly mounted sabers and fowling-pieces; laced hats and sumptuous garments of all sorts, with numerous other matters of European manufacture, were strewn about among greasy calabashes half-filled with *poee*, rolls of old tappa and matting, paddles and fish spears, and the ordinary furniture of a Tahitian dwelling.

All the articles first mentioned were, doubtless, presents from foreign powers. They were more or less injured: the fowling-pieces and swords were rusted; the finest woods were scratched; and a folio volume of Hogarth lay open, with a coconut shell of some musty preparation capsized among the miscellaneous furniture of the Rake's apartment, where that inconsiderate young gentleman is being measured for a coat.

The first Pomare, the most prominent chief of Tahiti, was known to Captain Cook as Otoo. Otoo was destined to become to the pagan world of the South Pacific what Constantine the Great was to pagan Europe. Otoo welcomed the first English missionaries to Tahiti in 1797, became their leading convert, and with their help acquired such an ascendancy over the other chiefs that he was soon declared king of all the Society Islands and their dependencies. Otoo changed his name to Pomare I, and by the time of his death in 1803 he had brought his entire kingdom of island subjects into the Church.

The rest of the Pomares were not quite so celebrated as their illustrious forbear. Pomare II fought a series of religious wars before death came in 1821. Pomare III was still a small boy when death took him. He was succeeded by his elder sister Aimata, who became Pomare IV and reigned from 1827 until her death in 1877. Because of conjugal infidelity, she was excluded from the communion of the Church. The back-sliding queen was succeeded by her son Pomare V, last king of the islands, whose reign ended three short years after his coronation. In 1880 his kingdom was formally annexed to France by a fleet of warships.

Papetoai Bay was as exclusive to the *Viator* as though we had sailed onto the waters of a mountain lake. Once at anchor, we gazed at the high surrounding volcanic peaks and in our solitude felt quite the owners of all we surveyed. By nightfall Harry and I had made everything shipshape, and Hazel was ready with our first cruising meal—creamed tuna and peas on toast, lettuce-and-watercress salad, and hot canned brown bread and jam for dessert. We ate with the appetites of young stevedores and were so exhausted from the excitement that no one thought to remark on the incongruity of opening canned tuna in the greatest tuna waters in the world!

Papetoai Bay isn't always quite the deserted spot we found it. Three mainland families, the Kellums, Wessels, and Philips, were usually in residence but we happened to call at a time when they were vacationing abroad. The bay was in the hands of a committee of one, the priceless Turia, *pareu*-clad and barefoot. At dawn of our first day she paddled out to bid us welcome and offer us the courtesy of showers and bed-rooms ashore. At her suggestion we raised our anchor and lay ourselves alongside the Philips' dock — a much more convenient arrangement than shuttling back and forth in our little punt.

Turia had been to New York, London, and Paris many times and had always returned gladly to the peace and security of her native soil — without the bobbed hair or French heels she could so easily have acquired.

We had heard something of her before we came: of her Pomare blood, her command of French and English, and her sparkling person-ality. But she was attractive beyond anything we had pictured.

After she had shown us the three bungalows of the landed gentry— her friends, all of them, who had asked her to be caretaker in their absence—we paddled around the bay shore to see her home. She and her brother had built all of it themselves, and it was the ultimate in pure native design. The house was in three units, kitchen, living room, and bedrooms, each with its floor of waxed maroon cement. The walls were of woven bamboo, the roofs of pandanus fastened by coconut-fiber thongs to the supporting *purau*-bough rafters. Matted bamboo blinds, swinging outward to the eaves, sufficed for windows. The furniture, each piece fashioned from native woods, was also their handiwork. Hand-dipped cushion covers in pastel shades harmonized with the floors and furniture.

When we admired a hundred soft hibiscus blossoms radiating from an end-table vase, Turia explained that the stems were twigs of the orange tree, and fresh flowers were carefully gathered each morning and stuck one by one upon the tiny orange thorns. As we chatted, she leafed carefully through a copy of *Vogue* we had brought her, and stopped at a full-page portrait of Lady Mountbatten.

"I guess the world is truly a small place after all," she said, reaching to a side table for an autographed picture in a silver frame. "Lady Mountbatten gave me this when I was in England two years ago."

Turia not only excelled as a housekeeper; she also was assistant breadwinner. While her brother worked back on the hillside with their breadfruit and coconut trees, she stalked fish in the front yard. Her routine was simple. First she went down the beach with a throw net, casting over schools of omas until a dozen or so were caught and transferred into a little floating bamboo cage. This, the live bait, she then towed behind her canoe to a favorite submerged coral ledge about 25 yards from shore. Making her boat fast with a stone anchor, she would then light a cigarette, and lower away the baited hooks. She told us she had yet to report a catchless expedition.

The following morning Harry and I put *Okay*, our little Marquesan outrigger canoe, in the water, and paddled to the head of the bay and up a lovely winding stream, the Oponu, that drains the verdant d'Oponu valley. The stream was so jungle-looking, so overhung with green branches and trailing vines, that we might have been in deepest Africa. Paddling slowly we passed a continuous floating procession of yellow and pink *purau* blossoms. At last we found a deep pool about a mile above the mouth, tossed our clothes over an abruptly leaning coconut tree, and had a swim—a refreshing change from the salt lagoons. Harry topped it off by walking, monkey fashion, up our clothesrack and hurling down drinking nuts — which tasted exceptionally good, either because of the primitive way they were obtained or the effort we had opening them with a pocket knife.

We felt so invigorated after our swim we decided not to return to the *Viator* direct but instead to paddle around to the pass and proceed along inside the reef to Paopao Bay. We had read of a deep cave that could be entered high up the face of one of Paopao's cliffs, and this was our sketchy excuse for going.

By the time we reached the head of the bay, we began to doubt whether we would make our destination by canoe. Outside the reef the seas were running much higher than usual, and the wind was so strong that quantities of spray were carried over into the lagoon, hitting our faces like hail. We found out later it was the first day of the *maraamu*, the cold wind that blows for a week every month. Gradually, as we worked around the land's end, the lagoon assumed a chop too steep for our little boat to ride, and we had to take turns bailing. This so slowed us that in an hour's paddling we had scarcely covered half the distance to Paopao; we therefore beached the boat and decided to proceed afoot.

One never reads anything about the abrupt changes of temperature which accompany the *maraamu*. Even the *hupi,* or night breeze, which comes down from the mountains each evening, making sweaters a necessity, has been kept secret by the sunny South Sea writers. It was fortunate that Harry and I had polo shirts along, for the farther we walked the more the cool wind bit us. Then, just as we came upon the bay, a replica of Papetoai, a warm rain commenced and we quickened our steps to find shelter.

A few native huts dot the beach at the head of Paopao Bay, and to serve them there is a ramshackle shed housing the inevitable Chinese store. By the time we reached it, the rain was coming down in the unreal manner of movie storms, and shelter was a necessity. We tried to make some inquiries about our mysterious cave, but the Chinaman gave every evidence of not having been outside the "store" since the day it opened — sometime in the '90s, to judge from the labels on the canned goods. By the time we had wrung out our clothes the rain had ceased, and we proceeded to find what the far side of the bay had to offer.

The sun reappeared and brought out the land crabs. We passed over thousands of their holes and played a sort of game, trying to overtake them before they could vanish at our approach. The faster we walked the faster wave after wave of crabs scurried to their retreats, where they paused for a second and slid slowly out of sight. At last, running as fast as we could, we managed to corner one. He was about as large as a saucer but an exceedingly fearless little fellow. Since he saw no chance to get past us to his home, he decided to fight it out, putting both claws up in boxing fashion. He snipped through good-sized twigs that we offered him as though they were straws.

While we were experimenting, a small native lad came up, put his bare foot on the crab's back and, grasping him just behind the claws, dropped him into a tin pail he was carrying. The lad had a long bamboo pole with a bunch of young palm leaves dangling on a string, and he set about showing us a more sporting method of catching land crabs. No fly fisherman at home ever cast a trout lure with greater accuracy than our lad exhibited with his bundle of greens. He would cast to a particularly large hole and move the lure slightly until a brown claw was firmly imbedded in it, then whip his pole up in the air, landing a crab at his feet. The meat of the land crab is a favorite native bait for lagoon fishing, and to the youth of Moorea falls the chore of keeping each family well supplied.

At the head of the bay we came across the Tahitian equivalent of a colonial quilting bee. The women and children of several families were gathered on the beach, putting the last touches on the weaving of a great coconut-leaf strip, four feet wide and fully a hundred feet long. The only man in sight sat on a stump by the road, a gray gull perched on his shoulder. Everyone called "iorana" (hello) to us, and the man laughed and made signs that we should sit down and watch the fun.

Soon a dozen buxom females trailed the primitive net out into the waist-deep water in a half circle. Then the children formed ranks between the beach and the ends of the net and sang and danced and splashed and screamed to drive the fish to the center. Pulling the tightly meshed matting closer and closer shoreward was no easy task, and the women strained like Volga boatmen against the weight of the water. At the finish of the haul they all joined—all but the lone male—in tossing their heterogeneous catch onto the bank.

At this point the gull left the man's shoulder and circled above the coconut tops, creeing and scolding until his master went to the catch and returned with a handful of small fish. The bird had evidently enjoyed the sport many times before, for he zoomed and snapped rhythmically as each morsel was extended to him. As we waved goodbye and started on our way, the women were tugging seaward to repeat their performance and our friend was rummaging in the community food for more morsels to appease his scolding bird.

Our efforts to find out anything about the cave were futile; we could make no one understand us. But walking back to the canoe without facing the downpour that had dogged us on the way over, we did considerable looking. One cliff behind the point of the bay nearest home looked likely and we resolved to return next day and try again.

That night, Turia was much interested in our exploits and we read to her a passage from Mulhauser, the renowned English deep-water yachtsman, which began: "On June 11, 1924, I sailed on to Moorea — one of the most beautiful islands, if not the most beautiful island, I have ever seen." And Mulhauser went on to tell of a tunnel that was supposed to run two miles under Mount Rotui, connecting Papetoai and Paopao

Bays. It had been dug in ancient times for use in case of hostile attack. He had found an entrance on the Papetoai side, a small opening through which he crawled. When he had proceeded several hundred yards into the mountainside he was stopped for lack of air and had to come out. The opening on the Paopao side was said to be taboo ground, for it contained a burial canoe in its entranceway.

Turia explained that the shaft on her side had been closed by cave-ins, but she thought we might find the entrance on the other bay. She offered to send with us a little neighbor boy, Timi (this was Timi II), if we really wanted to track it down. Timi could do two things, she explained: act as interpreter and warn us about landslides. The landslide matter was no joke; there had been so many heavy rains in recent weeks, especially on the Paopao side of Rotui, that we would be lucky not to run into a shower or two of falling rock.

Turia, in her musical voice, told us many things about her island. She spoke of the peak, Monaputa, which has a hole through it near the summit. According to legend the hole was made when the spear of a wrathful Tahitian god passed through, hurled from far-away Papeete. She spoke of Tohivea, the cathedral mountain, whose 4,000-foot spire looms like a skyscraper above the flooded craters of the two volcanoes that make up Moorea. Looking upward through the night to the grotesque peaks surrounding us, we could almost believe the tale about the god O-tu-one-iti. He was one of the youthful gods of ancient Polynesian lore. A builder god, he busied himself each night digging valleys and pushing up mountains. But he was also a highly vulnerable god, for he lived under a curse whereby, if at any time he should fail to cease his work before dawn, he would be forthwith changed into a *maoa.** This condition accounted, of course, for the unexpected landscapes on all sides. Often, of an early-morning hour, O-tu-one-iti would just be in the middle of rearranging a number of peaks, streams, and valleys. Then when dawn-time approached, catching him with an armful of mighty rocks ready to dump into the sea, he would drop everything where he stood and disappear into space until the following night. Of course, as he always arrived in the dark, it was impossible to pick up where he had left off, and his uncompleted efforts resulted in the higgledy-piggledy terrain.

A small shellfish.

On the flora and fauna side, Turia told us the natives used a special drug to stupefy certain kinds of fish and make for easy catching. When the nut of the barringtonia was grated and spread on top of the water, fish the size of mullets were rendered slow-moving and easy to capture. This fish narcotic was one of many herb and tree drugs that were used widely in olden times.

Turia spoke of one very unwelcome guest who had put in an appearance every day or so in her bay. This was a giant ray, that had somehow come in from the deep sea. This great flat fish, which she had nicknamed "Oscar," measured more than 20 feet across its back. Often it curved out of the depths of the bay in the dead of night, to shimmer a moment in midair, before crashing to the surface in an enormous belly-whopper, loud enough to wake everyone within hailing distance.

The bay was flat and black and still as we three paddled *Okay* back to *Viator* from Turia's beachfront. With only an inch of freeboard showing at our gunwales we were in no mood for anything that might disturb our trim. As we climbed aboard we opined that "Oscar" must have been preoccupied munching mollusks somewhere on the bottom shallows and we were glad of it.

The following noon Harry and I started our second conquest of Paopao, accompanied by young Timi, who proved to be a likable little fellow as well as a player of the harmonica. He knew two tunes: "Lafayette," a current Papeete hit, and "Hallelujah, I'm a Bum." But as guide, Timi was somewhat of a disappointment. After talking to some natives dwelling near the area where we thought the trail to the cave should start, in a gesture of despair he turned the lead over to us, or to Harry. Harry was one of those hikers who thrive on uphill work, and he forged ahead so fast that Timi and I soon lost sight of him in the jungle above. As there were no trails, we two simply kept climbing in the general direction of the foot of the cliffs.

After pushing through a layer of wet, low bush, interspersed with the usual thick growth of coconut, we came onto a slope of slippery rock and wet black topsoil. It was so steep that we fell down every few steps. A few hundred feet further on the smell of putrid fruit was added to our discomforts. We slipped and skidded upward through an area of rotted breadfruit that seemed never ending. There must have been enough squashed breadfruit on the ground to feed all of Moorea. The last lap was mostly jagged, crumbling rock, straight up and down in places, with *purau* growing everywhere, as well as some mango and a bearing wild papaya, of which we partook. At the foot of the cliff the trees were horribly mutilated and made one think of the trees on picnic grounds at home. But there were no initials or hearts carved on these: the butchering was all the result of rock falling from above. The limbs had been hacked off one side of a large *purau,* and a sharp rock the size of an anvil was buried in the trunk. I am sure this recalled to Timi's mind his responsibility to us in the matter of slides, for he studied the tree a long time before sitting down to mouth a chorus of "Lafayette."

Timi's air finished, we commenced working slowly around the base of the volcanic wall and eventually caught up with Harry. He had climbed a tall tree and seen a ledge which appeared to have something upon it. My ascent of the tree only confirmed my feeling that the sooner we got out from under the cliff the better. I *did* see what looked like the prow of a canoe protruding from the darkness of a recess in the rock, but looking higher I realized that it was just a question of time until the whole face of the cliff slid down. A ledge 500 feet above us looked as though it was only waiting for the laying of a sea bird's egg to start the avalanche. Just as I was scanning the skies for birds, Timi gave a shout and emerged from the recess, holding the so-called canoe out for our inspection. He had walked spider fashion from a point farther along, which was hidden from my line of vision, and had lost no time getting at the bottom of the mystery. The "canoe" was a crude box containing bones and fragments of tapa. We motioned to him to replace it and made haste to beat the darkness back to Papetoai.

Nightfall caught up with us halfway to Turia's. Timi and I began to drag our feet, but Harry forged ahead on the double quick. We had stopped and were listening to his pattering feet as they hit the puddles in the gloom ahead, when suddenly there was an extra-loud splash and all sound ceased. Harry had missed a bridge by ten feet and trotted into a neck-deep stream. We approached as he was pouring water out of his camera, but he quickly quashed any sympathy we might have had for him by trotting off again like a shot. If Harry hadn't set such a sterling example, I would have imagined we had been through a strenuous time. Timi and I were a mass of scratches from head to foot, and I had walked the tops out of a pair of tennis shoes.

Our last days in Moorea were spent in fishing with Turia, wild-chicken hunting, and designing a suit of sails for our outrigger, which Timi had begged us to rig for sailing. The sewing of the sails we turned over to a dear old soul near the village of Papetoai who had the only sewing machine for miles around. On the day Harry, Timi, and I called for the completed job, we found her seated upon the floor of her hut, her black Mother Hubbard in striking contrast to the white of the sails; she was reinforcing everything by hand as though her life depended upon it. Indicating we would be back in an hour, we strolled down toward the village, which turned out to be a few thatched huts and a small school.

As we looked upon the neat pile of salvaged *Kearsaint* cannon which the school children play upon in lieu of swings and acting bars, Timi sang a new song for us. It was a derisive bit of Tahitian jingle which kidded the French for running the *Kearsaint* on the reef in good weather and in broad daylight. A native composer had put the song together in a mood of pique after several weeks of hauling heavy cannon off the reef. The first verse translated into something like this:

> *Tane he sails a boat of wood,*
> *François an iron canoe;*
> *François he proudly hits the reef*
> *Tane goes safely through. . . .*

When we had returned to the little lady and her improvised sail loft, the sail was ready and she presented it to us with a large smile. She spoke no English but wanted us to know that we were welcome. She sent a grandson up a tree for drinking nuts, and while we were waiting she rummaged in an old sea chest and gave us each a stone adze—very old ones that had been picked up on her place in the course of years. After we had paid her a few francs for the sails, which she seemed sincerely reluctant to accept, she followed us out into the yard. Here a number of decayed canoes served as flower boxes, and she picked us a little bouquet to take along.

The afternoon we chose to leave Moorea turned suddenly dark and ominous. The surrounding peaks which we had admired on so many occasions were cloaked in mist; a great bank of black clouds closed in from the west as though to smother our attempt to reach deep water in daylight. (It didn't occur to us that with months at our disposal there was no need to sail off in a squall.) We had promised Turia to fly the blue peter when the boat was ready for sea and give her time to paddle across the bay and come aboard for a last farewell. It was 6:30 before we had put the deck in order, stowed everything below with extra care as a precaution against the weather outside, and gone over the charts and sailing directions for Huahine,* 97 miles distant. By 6:35 a sound as of two express trains racing in from the pass warned that a tropical deluge was pelting the palm fronds ten minutes away and would soon be upon us. We donned oilskins, kicked on the motor, and headed out, not pausing to do anything about the flag. Hazel made our farewell to Turia by semaphoring a flashlight from the companionway, and just as the heavens opened up, an answering light shone from the inky pocket to starboard.

Giving respectful sea room to the low bits of the *Kearsaint* faintly silhouetted against the murk, we slowly churned out into the wind, which by now was sweeping the valley in awesome gusts. This was a time when the little motor literally stood between us and trouble. Its throb couldn't be heard above the whine of the wind, so it felt as though some invisible force was carrying us through the pass. Once outside the reef, Harry and I jumped to putting the sails on as Hazel rounded the boat up into the wind. There was quite a little sea piling up, and as the sails thrashed and slatted and a couple of combers rolled aboard, I cursed the luck that I hadn't better memorized where everything was before this first night off soundings. I slid and ricocheted around on the water-slick decks in very lubberly fashion, admiring Harry's smooth know-how as we trimmed her down to the rail breeze that would put us off Huahine at dawn.

We traded watches through the night, and by 6:00 a.m., with Harry at the helm, all was peaceful and quiet in our bunks below. The skylight had been removed and the cabin was bathed in bright morning sunlight. The boat was riding smoothly now and flecks of clouds framed in the rectangle of sky above were torn bits of tissue paper that someone had tried to put together again. I looked across at Hazel's placid face, almost smiling in her sleep, and felt that if there were a Congressional medal for adaptability she should have one.

"On the road to Mandelay-ay-ay" floated softly down the com-

Hoo-ah-heeny.

panionway, calling me to the tiller. While Harry nimbly ascended the foremast, singing the rest of the song, squadron after squadron of flying fish hedge-hopped the blue waves to right and left. Huahine appeared at 8:00 a.m. as scheduled, but with a falling wind we still had several hours' sail to the entrance of the lagoon off Fare. Through our glasses we could plainly see the trees growing horizontally from the peak of Mount Paeo—as cryptically described in the *Pilot Book.*

Another climb up the mast had revealed a generous opening in the reef—a fairly straight passage across the lagoon to a tumble-down wooden dock, but as we swung to go in, the wind dropped to force zero and it seemed to take forever to ghost across the remaining half mile.

The Third Island—HUAHINE

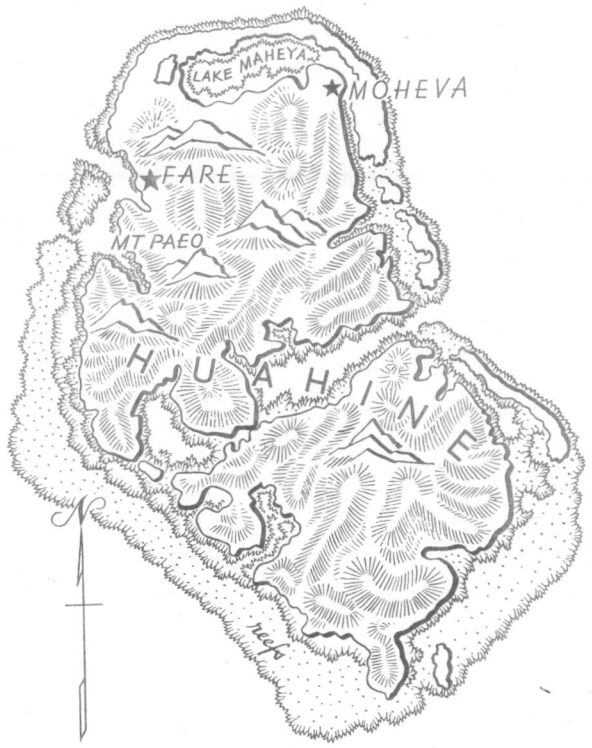

B Y THE time we had closed with the Fare dock a hundred or so natives, mostly children, were waiting to meet us and lend a hand with bumpers, lines, and sail covers. Some of the children lay on their stomachs opposite the stern trying to read our name.

"Vee-ate-or, Vee-ah-tor."

"Sahn-frahn-kisco."

All general talk was Tahitian but occasionally the words "yatch marite" could be heard. Any boat from the United States, regardless of size or cargo, is a "yatch marite" (American yacht) in French Oceania, and since Huahine hadn't seen one in over a year, we were a real curiosity.

At length a tall native with gray hair and regular features—the only human in sight wearing shoes—stepped aboard.

"Welcome to Huahine, my friends. My name is Chave, but everybody in Frisco called me 'Sonny.' I was two years a salad boy at the Clift Hotel. I am at your service."

"Can we buy some oranges and papayas?"

"No sooner said than done," and Sonny elbowed his way back through the crowd just as a European with a white waxed mustache appeared from nowhere and called to us in French suggesting we take the boat's papers around to the *préfet de police* for inspection. He vanished as suddenly as he had appeared, leaving us to figure out just where the *préfet de police* might hold forth. By the time we had our papers together, Sonny was back with a basket of oranges and said the papayas were on the way. There were exactly 100 oranges in the lot, and a native would be around sometime the next morning to collect five francs.

Following Sonny's directions to the *préfet de police,* we walked along the village path to a creek and on the other side brought up at a little building that seemed to be a combination school and sanctum of officialdom. Inside we were greeted by a lone official—the man with the waxed mustache. He shuffled through our papers without pausing to read anything and bowed us out—the whole operation not taking thirty seconds.

The Frenchman's attitude was that of an all-but-extinct type of colonial officialdom, but the friendliness of the natives on every hand was as genuine as the day the island was first claimed in the name of his Britannic Majesty George III. It was on July 15, 1769, that Lieutenant Cook had anchored his *Endeavour* a few yards from where we lay. The *Endeavour's* anchor had barely gripped bottom before the ship was boarded by a horde of enthusiastic, gift-bearing natives.

Probably no diplomatic conquest in British history was so easily concluded as was Cook's deal with King Oree. The Great Navigator simply stepped ashore and gifted the king with "a handkerchief, a black silk neckcloth and some beads . . . these ceremonies being considered a kind of ratification of a treaty between the English and the king of Huahine." To clinch the arrangement, the king gave Cook a hog and two bunches of feathers, and as far as the Lords of the Admiralty were concerned, the island was thenceforward British.

After a good night's rest we were early roused by Sonny and his *vahine* (wife), inviting us to join them in a visit to Moheva, ten miles north along the shore. It was Sunday and they had been asked to dinner at the chief's, who they said would be very happy to include us. They had arranged to go as far as the end of the road in a Chinaman's truck (the island boasted three automobiles) and the remaining few miles by canoe.

Our ride to the road's end was a memorable one for two reasons: it was the bumpiest we had ever experienced; and a severe case of elephantiasis rode with us. The unfortunate victim was a woman of about 50 and such was her condition that three natives had to lift her into the truck. Her trouble was concentrated in the right leg, which bulged at the ankle to the size of a wastebasket, hiding all the toes of her bare foot. To Hazel, Harry, and me, this spectacle was a jarring preliminary to a native feast, but everyone else took it for granted. Huahine was noted for fey-fey (elephantiasis), Sonny told us, and we might expect to see much worse. We had seen some elephantiasis in Tahiti, but nothing like this. According to one native theory, it came from eating overripe breadfruit at certain times of year. Only recently has it been confirmed medically that the disease is transmitted by the mosquito *Culex fatagans*. Sonny told us he had heard of tourists contracting fey-fey and losing it promptly upon their return to a temperate climate, but this sounded too simple to be true. We were glad when we parted company with our passenger at the canoe landing.

A half hour's canoe ride landed us at our destination, a thatched native village on stilts over the water, each house having its little thatched privy alongside.

The lagoon at this point is more in the nature of a salt-water lake: the barrier reef, two hundred yards to seaward, has in the course of centuries become what hydrographers called a "fringing reef"— solid land, heavily wooded. Because of this circumstance, Moheva is sheltered and very hot.

We caught the villagers just as they were returning from church in some very new-looking store clothes, and Sonny explained to us that the island was in the midst of booming vanilla prices and the natives were comparatively rich. The last schooner from Papeete had called but a few weeks before and brought bicycles, bureaus, bedsteads, and other badges of affluence which the natives readily purchased with the money paid them by the local Chinese vanilla magnates. The natives are particularly adept at growing and hand-pollinating the vanilla, which the Chinese buy and cure, and are all busy during a vanilla market.

There was but half a mile of path suitable for bicycling in Moheva, but every house had its shining vehicle out in front, and many of the churchgoers passed us rolling theirs along by hand.

The villagers' Sunday dress was fantastic. Bare feet protruded from under new suits and dresses, and shoes, dangling by the laces, were carried over arms. The women seemed partial to large straw picture hats, while many of the men wore felt berets of red or green. Although on week days *pareu* cloth reigned supreme, on Sundays during a vanilla boom the comfortable loin covering was considered out of order.

As we walked by the bamboo *himine*** house and looked in, we saw a few natives sitting upon mats on the dirt floor. The native preacher stood talking to some stragglers and pointing repeatedly to the book in his hand. His was the only complete ensemble in evidence—a white suit surmounted by a black bow tie. Huahine was one of the principal stations of London Missionary Society work in the early 19th century, and although there are at present no resident missionaries, the islanders still devoutly embrace the faith.

The chief's house was new—a wooden box twenty feet square, roofed with shining tin. It looked incongruous in the row of bamboo and thatch, but he was proud of it and there was no question but that it excited the envy of his subjects.

The chief and his brother were younger than we expected and were conservatively dressed for a Sunday in Moheva in khaki trousers and shirts. They were introduced to us, Sonny acting as interpreter, and immediately they set about showering us with hospitality.

Chairs and table were sent for and as we crowded into a little room over the water the chief appeared with a pitcher of punch. It tasted of rum together with fruit juices but the predominating flavor was vanilla, a vanilla pod being immersed in it. With the seven of us seated around the table and the punch poured, a dignified thanks offering was said and the meal started. The chief and his brother sat at the head, Hazel at the foot and Harry, I and the Chaves along the sides. Our hosts' women folk were never in evidence. They stayed in the cook house across the road and sent the food to the door by children from whom it was received and distributed by the chief.

There was cubed raw fish in coconut sauce, taro, yams, fei, hot bananas, breadfruit and suckling pig. Hazel and I were amused as we

---

*Himine, *pronounced* him-in-ee (*derived from English "hymn" singing*).

eagerly ate the raw fish to recall the things we had read concerning this Tahitian dainty. It has often been described as a shocking dish that one grows accustomed to gradually. If Sonny hadn't told us it was raw fish we would have thought it just an exceptionally tasty sea-food cocktail. Since the uncooked fish is soaked in lime juice and dipped in coconut cream before eating, it is not unlike a delicious marinated herring in cream. We ate all that was put before us and passed our plates for more.

We from the *Viator* ate with forks of very thin aluminum which promptly broke, one after the other, much to our embarrassment. Our friends ate with their fingers and saturated everything in bowls of coconut sauce before sucking it into their mouths. The sucking is an important part of native etiquette and signifies satisfaction. We were eating so silently amid the swish-swishing on all sides that at length Sonny announced that the chief's feelings were hurt. He thought we weren't enjoying things, and disappointment was written all over his crestfallen face. Sonny said if we couldn't suck we should say "maitai" (fine), every so often and thus raise the host's spirits. This we did, and soon the chief and his brother were beaming.

We were also advised to try to finish all the pork. Hot fish had not been served, being considered beneath our dignity, thus the young pig was a delicacy which we must relish. Everything was beautifully cooked by the old Tahitian method, modern stoves never having caught the fancy of the Huahinians. Only the ground oven, with leaf-wrapped food lying for hours under a pile of hot volcanic stone, can impart the flavor that permeated our perfect repast. We ate to the bursting point and even indulged in some finger swishing before we repaired to the porch and lay down for siestas on the sleeping mats.

After a suitable rest we were taken out to the "backyard," where the chief, through Sonny, explained the workings of the village fish traps. Centuries ago, in an era of civic planning, a maze of coral walls was built between Moheva and the fringing reef, so that transient fish might be diverted to shallow pools and scooped up at leisure. Succeeding generations have kept the project in working order, and today it is as much part of the community life as it ever was. The only improvement has been in the scoop nets, which now are often made of twine rather than woven bark. The abundance of easily netted food naturally explains the tendency to place fish well below pork on the bill of fare.

Moheva is rich in archeological remains, and on no other island were we to see so many of the great stone platforms, called *maraes*. Fifty yards from the chief's house stood one in a fair state of preservation. It was a rectangular wall of upright coral slabs, five and six feet high. In the center, over an area about 20 feet wide and 30 feet long, tons of coral lay loosely piled. Here, in ancient times, priests held important religious ceremonies, and occasionally human sacrifices were made to placate the gods of war and peace. Not far from this *marae* were the remains of a smaller one. It was almost completely grown over with brush, and a great *purau* tree rose majestically from its center, the green leaves and yellow blossoms striking a lively contrast to the gray of the stone. On one of the slabs were the faint tracery of several spiral figures and the outlines of a canoe. Since the old Polynesians had no written language, these engravings were particularly rare.

Near the church, a stone marked the resting place of Huahine's last king. A bottle embedded in its surface contained, for the sight of future generations, two of the king's teeth. To judge from the poor native teeth in evidence all around us, the old man must have been something of a specimen.

Across the lagoon and deep in the jungle growth of the fringing reef was a *marae* rarely visited by natives and scarcely ever seen by white men. As a special favor, the chief offered to take us to it. It proved to be well worth the hot walk. The structure was about 200 feet long and 15 feet high in places. Waist-high stone portals led into an antechamber. The interior of the *marae* proper contained literally thousands of large coral stones that, ages before, had been quarried from the reef. There were also many fragments of human remains. One skull particularly interested us because of the plain evidence of its owner's violent death. Some ancient stone cleaver had sliced away the bone so cleanly there was not a crack or a rough edge around the hole. Had we been on an unconducted tour, we would have lifted aside fragments of the rock and investigated further, but the chief was plainly uneasy and a touch superstitious of possible *tupaupaus* (ghosts) lurking in the vicinity; so we went back.

Around four we started for Fare, choosing to walk the shore rather than canoe to our Chinese taxi. It was a lovely walk over many good-sized streams, and at two of these we came on picturesque bathing parties. One was a very beautiful stream of swirling green water, in the middle of which a pair of smiling native girls sat on rocks and cheerfully greeted us. When we stopped for a picture, they laughingly struck poses and sang a song.

At the other stream, a more densely wooded one, two grandmas were sitting in the water and carefully drying a pair of tiny tots after having administered the daily fresh-water scrubbing. One of the children was white, and Sonny mentioned an American yachtsman as the father. He said there were several children on the island whose ancestry could be traced to American yachts, and the natives were rather proud of the fact. Extra children are always readily looked after by their grandparents, and white ones are highly prized in all families.

We shot some pictures here and so pleased the grandmother of the white child that she took us to her hut and gave us two pairs of mammoth blue crabs freshly caught in the lagoon. They were quite alive but so cleverly trussed up with bark thongs that only their eyes moved. When we parted with Sonny and his wife for the evening we cooked our crabs and sat down for the first time in our lives to more crab than we could possibly eat. The pieces of meat from the large claws were of the size of pork chops.

The days the *Viator* lay at Fare dock, with the exception of our visit in Moheva, were rather unpleasant. Our surroundings were far from beautiful after Papetoai Bay, and the crowds of children climbing around the deck and peering at us through the skylight became a decided nuisance. Had there been a way to anchor at Moheva we would have eagerly made the shift, but coral-glutted intervening shallows prevented it. We occupied the island's only practical mooring, and being dissatisfied there was but one thing to do—sail on. This we did, but not before a rather weird last night.

Just as we were preparing to turn in, a great wailing issued from a house not 20 paces from the dock. It was so loud, shrill, and persistent that we knew without being told that a death had occurred. Sonny appeared in a few minutes with the news that the oldest woman on the island had just passed away and natives would come for miles around to join the wake. Her death had been expected for some weeks, and relatives had even completed a sturdy coffin of native woods so there would be no delay after the spark of life had left the aged body. From our dock we could witness the whole proceeding, and since everybody appeared to be participating, we felt no qualms about looking on.

The one-room house was soon ablaze with coal-oil lamps, and against the blackness of the rest of the village it looked from where we sat like a stage set. Lamps lined the porch, and as more people arrived more lamps appeared. Through the large door and window could be seen the corpse propped up in a high bed with candles on either side. A tall preacher in white was gesticulating and shouting, but he could not be heard over the wailing.

Soon every inch of space on porch and steps was filled with squatting mourners, and groups began to collect in the yard. Of a sudden, as by previous arrangement, all wailing ceased and the preacher's voice rang out in a solo of musical Tahitian that lasted about half an hour. When he stopped, a multitude of women's voices filled the air in a very shrill chant that must have carried far out to sea. The sound could only be compared to bagpipes — a sound from human throats never to be forgotten.

The long sermon of the preacher apparently was the signal for a predetermined routine, because thenceforth through the night his talks and the chanting alternated at regular intervals. According to Sonny, some of the songs were Bible stories set to native music, and some were recently rehearsed songs concerning the deceased. All had been practiced at the *himines,* the weekly religious song fests of the church. He said he wished we had heard the singing at the *himine* house—it was considerably better and not characterized by the agonizing tones of the wake.

At 6:00 a.m. we sailed, and picking up the 15-knot trade outside the reef we soon put *Viator* beyond earshot of the Huahine funeral party.

The Fourth and Fifth Islands
–RAIATEA
and TAHAA

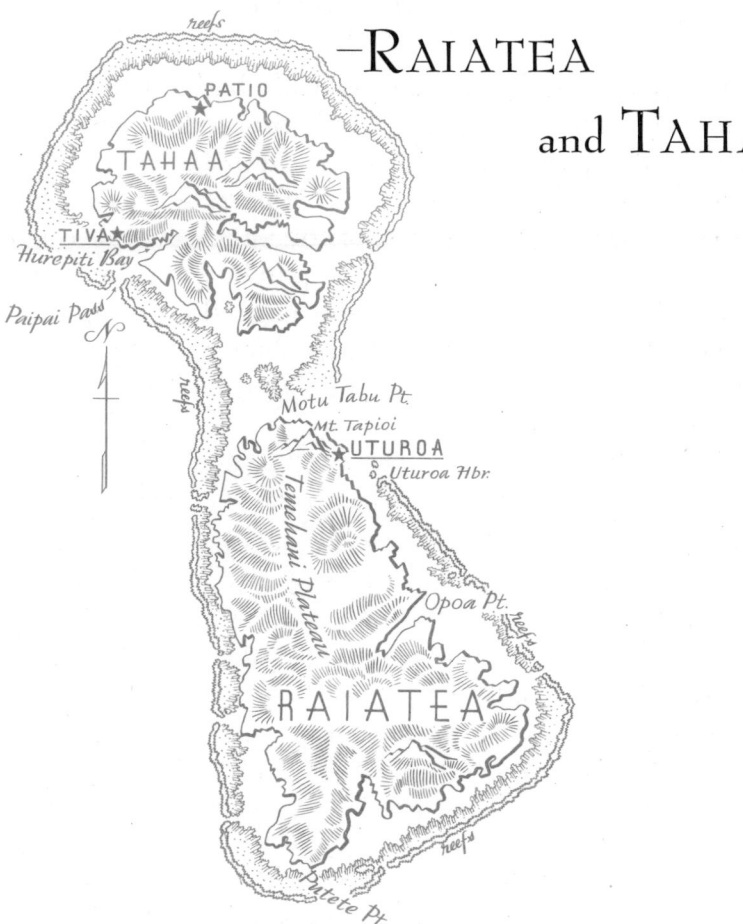

Good weather and a daylight sail brought us to a pair of islands we long looked forward to visiting. These, Raiatea and Tahaa,* lie twenty-five miles directly to the west of Huahine. They are unique in that both share the same submarine foundation and are encircled by a single barrier reef. Once inside the reef, one can sail from island to island without leaving the lagoon. Also the islands themselves are circumnavigable inside the reef; the continuous channel, shaped like a giant figure eight, is the only one of its kind in the South Seas.

In New York's American Museum of Natural History there is a very interesting relief map of Raiatea and Tahaa. It shows graphically the slow sinking of the two isles and the triumphant rise of the surrounding coral barrier. Looking at the sculptured map, one is very much aware

*Rye-uh-teé-ah, and Tah-hah.

that it is but a question of time until the volcanic cones disappear completely, eventually leaving a huge oval-shaped atoll.

The sea-flooded deep valleys and the scattered coconut clusters already growing on parts of the reef are clear evidences of what is going on. As we approached two of these clusters off Raiatea and looked beyond into an unusually deep bay, we felt we were witnessing one of nature's most remarkable metamorphoses. That the transformation may take several thousand years to complete in no way altered our feelings.

From the time we left Papeete, we had fallen back on our motor only once. We had resolved not to use it except when absolutely necessary, and were glad the prevailing trade wind would be strong enough to take us past the motus and through the narrow channel to the dock on sail alone. We had apparently been sighted miles out, for a galaxy of Raiateans were waiting to receive us, combined with a number of greeters who had sailed over from Tahaa for the occasion. The Tahaa people fascinated us as we watched some of their canoes flying across the lagoon as we came in. The sailing canoes of Raiatea and Tahaa are famed as the fastest native sail craft in the world, and out of the corners of our eyes we could see there was a busman's holiday ahead.

The slopes of Raiatea from the sea are most unexpected. Dozens of volcanic cones of all sizes break up any possible symmetry of the rolling hills. The whole thing looks as though Paul Bunyan tent poles of varying lengths support the terrain from underneath.

Uturoa, the little village next to our dock, sprawls at the foot of an especially jumbled mass of these cones, dominated by a prominent peak, Tapioi, which looks a great deal higher than it actually is. Before going in for canoe sailing, Harry and I climbed Tapioi's 968 precipitous feet and beheld an inspiring sight. Huahine lay gray and low on the eastern horizon. Bora Bora was a tiger tooth to the west, and a thousand shades of soapy-green lagoon squirmed between us and neighboring Tahaa. Harry, the real hiker of the party, disappeared over the summit before I had ascended halfway. We came together again for a few minutes as he returned, and decided the thing to do was to circumnavigate the island in a sailing canoe. The channel below looked so tortuous we knew that thirty miles of it couldn't help but challenge our sailing prowess. Later we would take the *Viator* over to Tahaa and spend a week investigating its bays and channels.

The matter of selecting a canoe for our round-Raiatea trip was fun. After wading the lagoon shallows and examining several of the visiting Tahaa craft, we proceeded to reconnoiter the beach beyond the town and study the local canoes propped in forked-stick cradles along the tree-shaded bank.

They were all pretty much alike in general characteristics — unchanged in design since time immemorial, but each had its fine distinguishing points. They averaged about twenty-five feet in length, and the log hulls were hand-hewn to an inch of thickness. Thong-laced planks extended the gunwales to an exaggerated height. The standard narrow beam, scarcely 12 inches on many, made the lines quite streamed when viewed from either end, and was of course a refinement made possible by the use of overdeveloped outriggers.

The favorite wood for hull and topsides was mango, the outrigger float being always fashioned of *purau*. Cotton-cloth sails had years ago taken the place of the ancient mat sails first seen by the missionaries, but for sail plan the style continued to be sprit main and no jib. Twisted-bark stays have not yet been replaced by rope, because rope doesn't stand comparison with the native product in either price or pliability. For us, the *pièce de résistance* of each rig was the steering paddle, and we were to learn that these are prized by their owners equally with the hulls. The word "paddle" is a misnomer—it is really a huge combination of lee-board and rudder, which is trailed near the stern at varying angles, depending upon the slant and strength of the wind. The "rudder" is from three to four feet in width and averages over six feet from blade-tip to phallic carving at the handle end. It is carved from a single piece of mara, and the width of the blade depends upon the size and shape of mara available.

Mara wood is hard and the grain runs in every direction, making it possible to shave the blade to unbelievable thinness without danger of splitting. Even so, it is wetted down each day and kept in the shade of the trees when not in use. In the next few years these distinctive, wonderfully hand-carved appurtenances will be replaced by some makeshift, for already the local scarcity of large-trunked maras has put a premium upon them, and importation of seasoned hard woods would be a costly impossibility.

The owner of the canoe we selected for our junket was Tuemata (meaning "eyebrows"). His canoe was fairly new and was beautifully made.

Hazel was elected to stay behind with the yacht while we circumnavigated. This assignment she took in good grace, and she saw to it that we had a well-stocked larder the morning of the take-off.

The most useful kitchen utensil in *Viator's* galley, according to Hazel, was a Montgomery Ward pressure cooker. The thing was a joy at sea, because it could be wired to the primus stove and no amount of pitch or roll would cause anything to spill. For our three-day canoe trip, Hazel pressure-cooked a gallon of Mexican beans, generously spiked with a canned ham and a pint of molasses. This, together with a few loaves of bread and a sack of fruit, we figured would be just about right. In fact ample, if Eyebrows was an average eater. If he wasn't we would spear a wild pig or maybe find a Chinese store and a couple of cans of sardines.

We took a trial spin over to Tahaa and back and were convinced that Eyebrow's craft wouldn't be overmanned with three of us. We took turnabout at the steering paddle, and such was the force of the lusty trade wind that two of us were constantly busy shifting our weight outboard and inboard with the puffs. On the starboard tack we perched on the outrigger beam, and on the port tack we perched on its continuation on the other side of the boat. It has been estimated that these canoes travel 18 to 20 miles per hour. I don't doubt that they will under perfect conditions, because we were doing around 15 in spite of our limited knowledge of the quirks of the boat.

We waved goodbye to Hazel and, finding the wind favorable for a counterclockwise course, headed around the northern tip of the island. Eyebrows timed things just right, and by twilight we were past Motu-tabu point. We spent our first night at the abode of Eyebrows' grinning brother, Timi III. Timi had been to San Francisco twice and spoke English. His trips to America had been as an able seaman on copra freighters from Papeete, and he had acquired a taste for Mexican chili beans. His women folk spread a table for us on the porch, and while they and the seven small children looked on, Timi, Eyebrows, Harry, and I ate most of our bean stew. Then Timi mumbled something to his oldest boy, a handsome chap of about eight, who scurried to the cook house and reappeared with an armful of bottles.

Each bottle had its cork laced on with a multiude of string windings, and in the yellow light of our single kerosene lantern looked quite mysterious. It was beer brewed from the papaya, and when our host unloosed the strings, corks flew in all directions. Harry and I drank sparingly, because we had sampled orange beer (sugar, orange juice, and yeast) in Tahiti and knew that all native fruit beers were dynamite. A normally kind-hearted native had wounded a friend with a machete blow to the head just before we left Papeete—a typical orange-beer-binge occurrence. But such is the influence of the church in these islands that native drinking is rare. Luckily there was only enough in Timi's cellar to emphasize his jovial qualities.

Timi and Eyebrows spent most of the time kidding about an occurrence that had taken place aboard the last American sailing craft that had called. This was the yacht, *Squally,* which carried four college boys from San Diego. One warm, dry day the skipper had himself hauled up the mast, looked it over, and decided that it needed a thorough coat of varnish. Thereafter for about two hours the boys took turns going up and down on a bos'n's seat vigorously applying the sandpaper until all was ready for the brush. Varnishing is always fun when a surface is well prepared, so there was some little argument as to who would have the honor of putting it on. The boys and the skipper matched coins and the skipper won. At about this point in the affair they all downed two bottles of papaya beer each. Up the mast went the skipper. Hoisted up after him went the "varnish." Only next morning was the awful mistake discovered. A perfect volley of curses roared from the deck as the skipper touched an admiring finger to the shining mast. It had been varnished with engine oil!

Around 9:00 p.m., having a big day ahead of us, we thought it was time for bed. We all dipped our feet in the five-gallon tin of water by the door, wiped them on a pile of rags, and entered the single room of the house.

On one bamboo wall hung the usual family bicycles, and on the wall opposite, the Sunday clothes of the entire family. Three mats with huge white pillows awaited us upon the floor of imported Oregon pine. Timi, his wife, and the seven children had their mats on the porch. The children were already asleep in various attitudes, while Timi's wife was still at the adjacent stream washing dishes. Our mats filled the floor space on one side of the room—on the other was a huge double bed with a canopy. Both spread and pillow slips were completely covered with a mosaic of embroidery. The bed, like the ones we saw in Moheva, had never been slept in or even as much as sat upon. It was perfectly new and unused. Timi patted me on the back and led me to it.

"You big fella—you sleep here. Maybe you like *vahine* too? I get you my cousin next door. Ve-ry good *vahine*. Ve-ry, ve-ry good."

"No," I replied, "Harry is the man for this bed—he is a bachelor and the logical one to accept your gracious offer."

Harry dived for a mat, turned over on his face, and went into a snoring act.. Then Timi made an effort to have me accept the bed without the *vahine*. But I couldn't bear to dishevel the family shrine. I joined Eyebrows and Harry on the floor and we bade Timi goodnight.

By 7:00 a.m. the following morning we were loaded down with gift bananas and coconuts and were ready to start. We had joined the family in a bath at the stream, eaten a bowl of raw fish, and paused only to examine a *nohu* one of the children brought in on the end of a spear. The *nohu* is supposed to be a great delicacy when properly cooked but is the ugliest thing imaginable to look at. This one was of about the same size and appearance as a headless plucked chicken.

Timi told us of a neighbor who had died as the result of stepping on one. Unless a *nohu* wound is immediately scarified and sucked, bed-ridden days of fever and terrible pain set in before death takes place. Once more we resolved to wear tennis shoes for the remainder of the voyage. As we pushed the canoe to deep water, Harry and I behaved as though we were walking on eggs. Eyebrows was disgusted with us and dragged his bare feet through the water with emphatic carelessness.

This day, we put in to shore at every opportunity. We called on the artist Jan Gouv, whom we had heard referred to in Papeete as the "Dutch Gauguin." He had 15 or 20 canvases on hand. Native dancers, canoes, and sunsets predominated. Gouv, like Gauguin, had left his native land (Holland, we were told), to live in a South Sea hut and paint, but there the parallel ended. Gauguin's natives were at least recognizable as natives but Gouv's were of the smudge school and rather unsettling to look upon.

He certainly had solitude in which to work. Although he was the tenant of a scant hectare of land at the head of a small cove, no other abodes marred the shore in either direction and he was master of it all. We were glad to see that he was more of a businessman than Gauguin. The immortal Paul traded his canvases for rent and groceries, little dreaming of the $50,000 price tags destined to dangle from them as years later they changed hands among the Paris dealers. Gouv's were all tagged with modest prices.

At Gouv's we heard the tragic story of Emile, a 22-year-old Swiss who went to Rurutu, down in the Austral Islands, to satisfy *his* Gauguin instinct. He had toiled eight months and had a dozen canvases to show for his pains when the Rurutu Christmas season rolled around. Being the only white man on the island, he was in great demand as a holiday dinner guest, and every family invited him to sit with them on Christmas day. He thought he had declined all save one invitation, but as he finished a bounteous feast at the board of his choice he suddenly recalled another family with whom he had promised to dine. He took a final helping of manioca, excused himself, and hurried to the other house. There, being a polite person, he again ate enormous helpings of breadfruit, fei, and manioca.

He returned to his bed that night feeling groggy. There was no doctor or stomach pump on Rurutu, and his European stomach couldn't absorb the overdose of starches. Two days later he was dead. The natives gave him a dignified burial and loaded his worldly goods, including the dozen canvases, on an interisland schooner for Papeete, where everything would be forwarded to relatives in France as addressed. The schooner was one of seven which foundered in the Tuamotus that particular year. The boat went down in deep water and all worldly effects of Emile with it. The fates had wiped him and his works from the face of the earth.

The bay of Monsieur Grojeant was our next stop. Here was an original Frenchman. His was the only elevated house we were to find until we reached the English settlements in Rarotonga of the Cook group. Everybody so far had lived on the fringes of flat land next to the beaches. Grojeant's house was perched on a hilltop—he had the only high view in the Society Islands. Eyebrows balked at going ashore. He said, *"Tabu-popaa,"* and we had to take charge of the canoe almost forcefully to keep from sailing by.

We had heard about Grojeant. He was Raiatea's utility magnate, and his coconut-husk-fed steam plant turned the generator which supplied the dozen or so electric lights in the village of Uturoa. His monopoly had thrived for years, and now he lived in retirement, letting a native engineer keep the plant going while he puttered on his estate.

Eyebrows behaved as though we were certain to be shot on sight. He never budged from the canoe as we went ashore and up to the door of a house on the beach. Machinery was buzzing noisily inside, and we knew our knocking couldn't be heard above it. We turned the knob and went in. In the midst of spinning wheels and whirring belts and pulleys stood a youngish shirt-sleeved Frenchman throwing a large switch open and shut at measured intervals. He looked up, cut a master switch, and came over to greet us, smiling and wiping his hands.

It was Grojeant, and he enjoyed immensely the fact that we had come in over the *tabu* warning. His habit of working alone everyday had earned him a reputation among the natives as a bit of a mystic. They couldn't understand why a man should tinker perpetually with machinery when he had enough money to go back to France and live in what they conceived to be luxury.

Grojeant's hobby was electrifying his home, and all his energies went in that direction. He showed us a shining generator whirring from the harnessed energy of a waterfall. From it he ran his lights, ice box, stove, vacuum cleaner, and many other electric gadgets. His greatest achievement, however, was but half finished: an incline railway from the beach up to his house on the hill. This too was to be run from the hydroelectric plant. The track was all but complete, and the parts for the cars were on their way from France. He apologized that it wasn't finished, and invited us to walk up the hill and meet his wife. But we were afraid Eyebrows might have gotten his wind up by this time, and we hastened to get back to the canoe. Promising our South Pacific Thomas Edison we would come back again if it could be arranged, we went on our way. Eyebrows was quite taken aback by our unruffled reappearance and our stock went up with him on the spot.

Down the leeward side of Raiatea we sailed, with at times hardly a breath of air reaching us over the island's continental divide, 2,500 feet skyward. Eyebrows seemed half asleep at the steering paddle, while Harry and I lay prone along opposite sides of the outrigger brace. This brace is scarcely eight inches wide, but so smoothly did our canoe glide in the light breeze I discovered I could doze off with equanimity, steadying myself in my sleep by only a finger hold on our braided outboard stay.

This was relaxation of a new sort. I could gaze for an hour at lofty green peaks shifting inch by inch astern, or focus half-closed eyes downward and be hypnotized by the procession of coral hulks and bright flashing fish forms below. For long periods our hull might ride but half a fathom over growthy bottom, now and again breaking branches from tree coral foolhardy enough to rear its brittle limbs in our path. Such depths would be crystal clear, and each stripe of tiny fish might be noted with ease. Then, of a sudden, bottom would drop away in alarming fashion changing schools of liveried fish into scattered handfuls of confetti, and feathery coral into vermiculated forms which quickly lost identity in the increasing murk. Our craft then became a glider, leaving Grand Canyon walls behind to soar over bottomless valleys of blue black.

There was no doubt about the sense of humor lurking deep in Eyebrows' soul. Only once that day were Harry and I both asleep at the same time, and it was too good a chance to let go by. *Thump!* The bow went up against a huge chunk of coral and plop, plop, Harry and I rolled off our narrow perches into the water. The boat wasn't moving fast enough to hurt anyone—the impact was only enough to dislodge us. But it was a good thing it happened, for on shaking ourselves and getting underway we looked about and saw some excitement ahead.

We were around Putete Point, the southernmost tip of the island, and a large bay spread before us, on the surface of which a flotilla of sail described a pattern. We had some breeze now, and by the time we reached the bay it was fairly brisk. A native regatta was in progress. Six canoes were sailing around a triangular course marked by stakes, and at the finish, opposite a village ashore, floated a large dugout at anchor. This was the "committee boat," and three natives sat in it viewing proceedings. We beached our canoe and joined the crowd on shore. We discovered this was an elimination to decide which boat should be chosen to represent the island at the mid-July Bastille celebration in Tahiti. The fastest canoe and crew would be shipped by schooner to Papeete, where it would perform before the governor and enjoy the hospitality of "la Perle du Pacifique." This was all explained to us by an old native who had seen the *Viator* at Uturoa and hailed us as we appeared upon the scene. We sat on the yacht-club verandah (porch of the Chinese store) until all the craft had finished, then made our exit as the winning crew took its bows.

After leaving the regatta we had a taste of real sailing. We lashed along for half an hour under a beam wind so strong the outrigger was out of water most of the time. A nasty chop added to the excitement, and it seemed that every other second our bow dove through it rather than over it. While Harry danced on the strut to windward, parrying the puffs, I crouched forward and used a small spare paddle as a pry to throw the bow suddenly to port or starboard when coral heads rushed toward us. We had many narrow sqeaks, but Eyebrows at the steering paddle didn't give up until we crunched viciously over two coral heads in succession. Then we came about and raced back to deep water.

With darkness the wind lightened and was blowing in our faces. We couldn't tack back and forth over the shallows, because coral hazards were no longer visible and our jibless rig was anything but ideal for windward work. We had to stay in the narrow channel and proceed slowly. We got out a couple of small paddles and took turns paddling.

It was our plan to put in at Opoa, spend the night there on a native porch, and go exploring first thing in the morning. We might even find a native family who would fix us some food, since the last of our beans had been eaten at Timi's and we had been living on coconuts and fruit ever since. Opoa, apart from the possibility of affording a change of diet, was the site of Taputapuatea, the great master temple of Polynesia. From this *marae* stemmed lesser *maraes* through island groups to the north, south, east, and west.

We emphatically did not want to miss Opoa, and we relied on Eyebrows to guide us there in the darkness. Time after time he assured us that Opoa was the next point ahead. By the time we had paddled by seven points—and it was a good mile between points—and Eyebrows for the seventh time had scrutinized the dark shore and indicated "one more point," we took the controls away from him. We made him stand in the prow and pry us through the coral hulks while Harry and I paddled the canoe to the beach. We left Eyebrows there and went along the shore to investigate.

We found we were just inside the mouth of a deep bay, and we could see a lone light flickering far along the shore. We walked down the beach half a mile and came to a little frame cottage. A shout brought an elderly Frenchman hobbling to the door. He held a lamp high which threw a light on his face, and asked us in imperfect English what was the matter. We explained that we thought it might pour during the night and sought some kind of roof for shelter. He said we could sleep in his "other room"— it had no bed but he would spread mats. Come in and see, he said.

Once inside, we had a rude shock. The Frenchman didn't hobble from age—a more evenly distributed light showed a pair of fey-feyed limbs fully as monstrous as the one we had seen on the woman in Huahine. He dragged his legs as though they were in immense plaster casts, and sat down with great difficulty.

Once outside again, we decided unanimously that the place to sleep was by the canoe. We spread palm leaves on the sand and the three of us rolled up in our mainsail, with the heavens for shelter.

We awoke on hallowed ground. One could have tossed a sea biscuit from our canvas bed to the famous crowning stone of Opoa. This pillar of sandy stone, half again higher than a tall man, was said to have been planted upon living warriors—their crushed remains were pinioned in the earth as voluntary sacrifice to Oro, God of War. This was in remotest antiquity, hundreds of years before the missionaries came and ruled out Oro in favor of our white man's God of Love, peace on earth, and friendship among men of all races and creeds.

The natives were more than glad to try the new idea. They agreed that their tribal wars, however small and infrequent, were shameful and had to stop. They lived up to their word and thus became part and parcel of the "great family of civilized races who love each other." They embraced the Christian ideal so wholeheartedly the *marae* was left to become overgrown with trees, and the crowning stone, where many a Raiatean sovereign had been proclaimed, was henceforth avoided like the plague. Recent generations of Raiateans know as little about the historic monument as native New Yorkers know about the Statue of Liberty. Eyebrows had never before seen it, and we already had ample proof of his sketchy ideas as to its location. For him, a legend had come to life, and he examined the surrounding jungle like a bird dog, calling us to every pile of rock he stumbled upon.

By midmorning we were on the last lap of our canoe cruise. A vertical rain dispersed any possible breeze and we paddled again, covering half the distance to Uturoa before it let up. The loveliest sight of the circuit appeared in the last few miles. Here the mountainous ridge ran along as level as though some prehistoric god had taken a plane to it. Cliff tops high above us were interspersed every few yards with wispy waterfalls, distinct in spite of their half-mile elevation. The water flowed from the great Tamehani Plateau, which was hidden from our view. What notoriety would this ridge of falls receive were it in America! One could visualize the ribbon of concrete leading motor cavalcades to its base, and the "natural amphitheatre" built in its shadow.

Back in Utoroa, we found a note on *Viator* telling us Hazel had moved to the village in our absence. Looking for more luxurious quarters, she had engaged a room in one of the most colorful hostelries of the South Seas, L'Hotel du Tapioi du Raiatea. Her boudoir, on a rickety second-floor balcony, was something out of a stage set for "Rain." The large four-poster bed, with overstuffed mattress of kapok, just about filled the room. Over the head of the bed was an ornate embroidery in a frame two feet wide and four feet long. It was an American eagle in faded red, white, and blue silk, and from its beak flowed a scroll, lettered "Welcome Dewey—hero of Manilla Bay."

Ragged brown-velvet draperies, that had long since lost the rollers and pulley to draw them closed, hung by the sides of the open balcony doors. For privacy, Hazel pinned them together with snap clothespins she had brought from the boat. The room was lighted with a kerosene lamp, which sat on a velvet-covered orange crate. Some oil-painted flowers on the frosted shade spelled out "Vive la France." L'Hotel du Tapioi du Raiatea left a memory of night noises with a sort of unending cadence heard in one's sleep: a bicycle bell, seemingly at half-hour intervals; the tattoo of rain on the tin roofing overhead; the unsteady groan of the coconut-husk power plant next door; natives in the kitchen below singing far into the night; a crying baby; a ukelele strumming somewhere across the road; a dog barking, and roosters crowing to be answered from far-away Tahaa. And at dawn the sandpapering sound of a youngster sweeping the street with a palm-frond broom.

Tahaa, the adjacent island, is fifteen miles around and almost circular in shape. The lagoon channel is deep, and *Viator* did it under sail. We took turns standing on the bowsprit and signaling Hazel at the helm, and once in awhile Harry climbed the foremast and waved directions. Halfway across, the sails went limp, and suddenly the lagoon surface became as smooth as a glass table top. Then the rain came down not in drops but as rods of water, making millions of miniature fountains on the surface around us. So much water came down in about 20 minutes that we plugged up our self-bailing drains and let the cockpit fill deep enough so that we could scoop the water up in bucketfuls, which we saved for washing. As suddenly as the rain had started, it stopped, and the breeze came back to push us along as before.

We tied up a few days at Patio, halfway around Tahaa, and played our phonograph continuously for a perpetual audience gathered at the little jetty. They liked our Hawaiian records best, and two local guitar experts had us repeat "Little Grass Shack" again and again to enable them to memorize the parts.

At Tiva, five miles farther around, we undershot the tiny pier as we came about into the wind, and before we knew it we were blowing against beach coral. We turned the motor on, pulled sail down with boat-drill efficiency, and backed off none too soon. Then a roly-poly character came out to us in a canoe and introduced himself as Old William. He spoke a little English and piloted us around to Hurepiti Bay and an unruffled cove. There he dived around the boat like a walrus, saw to it that a bow anchor was secure in the coral bottom, then swam two stern lines ashore to coconut trees. He also spent an alarming length of time under the boat, inspecting every plank to see if coral had scratched away copper paint when we swung into the beach. If any wood were bare below the waterline we would be vulnerable to teredoes, the same notorious tropical wood worms that riddled the planking of Columbus' ships while he was prowling for gold along the east coast of Panama.

The bottom paint was intact, said Old William. I "double checked" it with a fast dive along the keel and came up sputtering — my diving goggles full of water.

Old William was over fifty, fat, and wore only a loin cloth. He was a real suburbanite and sailed over to Raiatea but once in a great while on copra business. He owned a good-sized plantation, and our mooring trees belonged to him. He had a huge family of married sons and daughters, all of whom lived together in a thatch community surrounding William's house. Soon they began to appear upon the scene, only to be ordered off on various missions by William. The orders, we discovered, were all in our behalf. Some of William's family reappeared with baskets of oranges, some with bananas, some with coconuts. Most overwhelming of all, a son, Timi IV, in a canoe loaded to the gunwales with avocas (alligator pears), slid alongside and presented them to us. We tried to call a truce but got nowhere until our cockpit looked like a market stall.

There was to be dancing in the streets, or rather the paths, at William's after dark. We promised him we would appear sometime after supper and sent him off with a quart of rum under his arm, in answer to his request for some "lum for lum punch."

The moon was out at seven when a little boy called at the boat to guide us through the coconut trees to the impromptu carnival. The little fellow insisted on carrying our phonograph, which was too heavy for him but made him feel quite important. He put down his load only once, and then to pause on a moon-bathed promontory and scurry among some tree bushes for three *tiare** blossoms with which to adorn our ears. The fragrance of this flower is world renowned. Voyagers have sung its praises since earliest times. The correct name, *tiare* Tahiti, does not mean blossoms are to be plucked only on the famous isle. They grow on all the high islands of the Society group and even on some of the wooded atolls. The white satiny petals and lacquered leaves of the *tiare* are strikingly similar in texture to those of our domestic gardenia. The petals are seven in number, narrow, and rather waxy. Occasionally eight petaled flowers are found, and these are in great demand as lucky pieces. The perfume of the *tiare* is heavier and headier than that of most island blooms, and when a hundred of them are strung together in a lei they all but cause the wearer to suffocate in the concentration of fragrance.

When we arrived at the clearing in the palms which was William's "village green," we found about 40 natives sitting around in a circle, singing. The nearly full moon lighted the scene so well that no lamps of any kind were necessary. In this unreal atmosphere a little girl

*Tee-ah́-ray.

[72]

stepped forth and presented us each with frangipani necklaces. We would have preferred simply to sit and listen to the singing, but our phonograph was to be the star performer for the first part of the evening. They wanted more and more of our records, and only when we had repeated "Valencia" a dozen times did several of the men join the circle with guitars and the dancing begin.

We all danced, and only after the moon went down did the party start to break up. One particularly pretty young woman held a child of doll-like beauty in her arms and swayed with the music as the little girl blinked hour after hour to keep awake. Finally Hazel took the baby in her lap, and as the little thing slept, her *pareu*-clad mother did a most graceful hula. As for the rum punch, only old William and a couple of his brothers-in-law seemed to have very much. They became so pleasantly tipsy early in the evening that there was not enough left to affect anyone else.

The walk back to our mooring was in inky darkness, and we had a slight calamity as we set out from shore to board *Viator*. We had rigged our "sensitive" punt on a trolley arrangement to pull ourselves to and from shore without using paddles. In the darkness, Hazel and I had shuttled about halfway out when our ferry slipped from under us and we had to swim to our mother ship. Fortunately we had the stern line to hang onto, and fortunately the victrola was still on the beach with Harry when we capsized.

Our "shooting" of the narrow Paipai pass en route through Tahaa's reef to the sea was a real roller-coaster operation. The channel is over a thousand yards long, and sometimes an unbelievably heavy swell builds up in it. Our four-cylinder power plant conked halfway through the pass, but luckily we had the sails up at the time (a formality we had almost postponed). We sailed through the remaining 500 yards of pass and through the upper stories of high rollers, which sent fire-hose streams into the cabin before we could close the forward ports.

The Sixth and Seventh Islands
—BORA BORA and TUBAI

T HE famed "gay, laughing, singing, dancing natives" of storybook, Bora Bora greeted *Viator* with breath-taking enthusiasm. They boarded us before our anchor dropped and carried off dresses, shirts, pants, and shorts until we lost all track of personal belongings in the excitement. However, they did it all with our approval. Several canoes came alongside with grass skirts and carved things to sell. I offered a polo shirt in exchange for a skirt and decorated headdress. The deal was made, and Harry and Hazel immediately jumped on the bandwagon. There was never a dull moment after that until darkness closed in, making it difficult to see what was being exchanged for what. Not many days later I discovered that Hazel had assumed the wifely prerogative of trading off her husband's things with such complete abandon that I had to borrow from Harry's wardrobe for the remainder of the trip.

Bora Bora, or Bola Bola—or Vavau, as it was called in ancient times, is a kind of Moorea in miniature. It is actually fewer miles around than Tahaa, yet one would swear it was twice as large. This is because of its abrupt central peaks, Pahio and Temanu, 2,165 feet and 2,379 feet high, respectively. They are two gargantuan teeth, an eyetooth and a molar side by side, with sheer walls which, when viewed from a distance seem to drop to sea level. A barrier reef plentifully sprinkled with wooded motus encircles the island, and on the southwestern corner is Teavanui Bay, flanked upon the reef side by Tupua, a fairly high, wooded islet. Bora Bora has but one pass. This is around the northern tip of Tupua and leads to the bay just mentioned, being wide enough and deep enough to allow large ships to enter.* Coral shoals prevent any such thing as circumnavigating either Bora Bora or Tupua, but the fine bay offers a world of small-boat sailing. We sailed our little *Okay* with her new sails until we tired of it, then turned to native boats, which are much the same as Raiatea's sail canoes.

Only two white men were in residence when we arrived—the French administrator and the village schoolmaster. We had some Raiatea mail for the schoolmaster, which pleased him, but we depressed him when we begged off card playing. He and the *préfet* had been wishing for a "third and a fourth" for bridge, and when we sailed in they assumed we were the heaven-sent answer.

As on all the French islands, the teacher's job was to try the impossible: to train the children to speak French, in the hope it would eventually supplant the Tahitian tongue in every home. The crusade wasn't working any better in Bora Bora than it had in Raiatea, Tahaa, Huahine, Moorea, or Tahiti. The Tahitian language is as living a language as it ever was. Not one word of French did we hear from native lips except in the schoolyard. When we walked across the yard at recess time we were always greeted by a chorus of "Bonjour Mssrdames," run together and chanted parrot fashion. On the trails and by-paths the greeting of children was always "ioranna," pronounced "yah-rah-nah," with rising emphasis on the "nah" in imitation of their elders. It was quickly apparent that visitations of American yachts had made more of a dent on the native tongue than had the French school. Many of the natives spoke a smattering of English, and quite a few more could understand us even though they couldn't communicate too well in return.

---

*Bora Bora was the only one of the Society Islands to feel the impact of World War II. Allied shipping used the harbor as a rendezvous when passing from Panama to the war zone, with the result that between 1942 and 1945 there were 157 white babies born. After normal primitive conditions were restored, native divers reclaimed 53,000 "coke" bottles from the lagoon floor.

The big thing that was news about Bora Bora was its movie palace. A movie impresario in Papeete had long been aware of the thrifty character of the Bora Borans and realized something could be done about it. He knew they were unique in their energy: they sent more curios, copra, and vanilla on the trading schooners to Papeete than did most other native island communities, and they didn't dissipate so much money on bedsteads and gadgets as they might have done. They didn't even squander their affluence on Papeete clothing. Constant barter with yachts had given them more clothing than they could use. So the movie impresario built the Casino de Bora Bora, installed a gas-lit projector, and put a couple of Papeete-trained natives ashore to run pictures once a week. He returned to Papeete with a mint on his hands. A couple of ancient silent pictures, bought for a few dollars in America, were the whole bill of fare. These, alternated show after show while we were there, drew packed houses. If you referred to Betty Grable or Gary Cooper on Bora Bora you spoke an unknown tongue. Mention Anita Stewart or the late Ruth Roland, and you were right in the swim.

Ruth Roland, star of the early silent days, was the current attraction in Bora Bora. We saw her in "The Timber Queen"— all episodes rolled into one — and it was a unique experience. "The Timber Queen" was one of the breed of silent weekly-serial thrillers which sent the youth of another generation home to nightmares on Thursday nights, wondering whether the following week the heroine would be sawed in two or be saved by Jim, the Lumberjack. "The Exploits of Elaine," "Perils of Pauline," "Hazards of Helen," and "The Million Dollar Mystery" were all from this same rubber stamp. One rarely saw either a first or a last installment. But how memorable were those intervening episodes — beginning with pictures of the characters and a short synopsis of the plot, and continuing with ten minutes of action which was obliterated at a breath-taking moment by the announcement: "To be continued at this theatre next week."

The path to the Casino de Bora Bora was alive with activity on movie night. By a dozen lantern-lighted tables native vendors sold cuts of watermelon, rubbery coconut cake, and peanuts imported from Papeete. Much of the bartered finery was in evidence — ensembles as mixed as one could imagine. Groups came down the road singing softly to guitar accompaniment, and every man, woman, and child was bedecked with flowers. Some wore necklaces of flowers, some flower garlands around their hats, and all had either a hibiscus or *tiare* over the ear.

Outside, we talked to several whom we knew, and Ituri, whose *vahine* makes the loveliest grass skirts on the island, introduced us to all his relatives. Eleven were in his party, and he had bought tickets and watermelon and peanuts for them all with the proceeds from his wife's handiwork. He was glad of the weekly movie, he said, because there was nothing else to do with the money. He was a fine fisherman and lucky at raising pigs, and the family had never wanted for coconuts, bananas, and breadfruit, which grew on his land to excess. He had always contributed more than his share to the yearly London Missionary Society collection, and now the movies provided a good outlet for his surplus.

Inside, the Casino was like the inside of a small barn. There was a little sheetlike screen at one end and a boarded-up booth at the other for the shaft of projecting light. Long planks resting upon boxes were the seats, and smooth white coral pebbles the flooring. The air was clean and gently fragrant from the flowers. (There are no cleaner people on earth than the natives of these islands. Either they have showers rigged up in their yards—the water being piped through bamboo stalks from hillside basins; or they bathe two and three times a day in the streams.) There seemed about as many youngsters in the audience as grown-ups, but they were well-behaved and made less noise than their parents, who did a lot of peanut cracking and chatting before the picture began. Many of the men held their children on their laps, and several women had babes in arms who were complacently breast-fed throughout the evening.

About twenty episodes of "The Timber Queen" danced by one after the other, each episode crammed with fights and hair-breadth escapes. Ruth Roland crossed and recrossed the Yukon country a dozen times, but always the dynamited bridge over the turbulent stream blew up *after* her dog team had passed over it. She was trapped in the subterranean stronghold of a leopard-skinned, bushy-bearded hermit for at least three installments, yet every time that he pushed her into a cave annex filled with lions, she climbed to safety.

When the water reached her ears as she struggled for release from her cabin on a sinking ship, someone chopped an exit for her through the ceiling. She quelled a mutiny, threw a ferocious bull, and disposed of Manuelo, the best swordsman in the Argentine, with equal ease.

Some episodes appeared out of sequence — Ruth would be on the point of burning to death in a smoke-filled room, only to be saved at the start of the next installment from a mine cave-in. This was probably because much film breakage through the years had resulted in mixing up the picture and the Papeete impresario never bothered to re-edit the film. He might at least have taken out some of the painful reintroductions of characters. Seeing a stupid face leering just once from such a title as:

PINE PEAK HOGAN PROPRIETOR OF THE PINE PEAK DANCE HALL, A SQUARE SHOOTER AND OTHERWISE

is bad enough, but when same is repeated twenty times during the screening of a picture, even a nonreading native becomes restive.

In Papeete, a native interpreter shouted a translation of English titles into Tahitian, but in Bora Bora the audience was left to work things out unaided. However, they primarily loved action, and such was the action of "Timber Queen" that the titles were no great worry.

Early in the picture, "Knock Out" Hensen hit a seaman so hard the fellow broke the railing of a ship and dropped overboard. This started the audience yelling and cheering, and they never stopped until the picture ended. Then they were let down as were we. Ruth was hanging over a cliff on a slender rope while two men fought high above her. The hero wanted to pull her up, the villain wanted to let her go to a cruel death. Meanwhile, the rope, which was tied to a tree, was being worn through strand by strand as Ruth swung from it far below. We became dizzy as the camera went from close-ups of Ruth's anguished face to close-ups of the parting strands of rope to close-ups of the faces of the battlers on the cliff top. There the picture ended. Probably there is no such thing as the conclusion thriller — probably none was ever made.

We grew very attached to Ituri. He had as big a supply of clothes as anyone on the island, but most of his things were kept on hangers, to be looked at rather than worn. His suits, overcoats, and sweaters expressed every whim of fashion. He did make use of a pair of highly prized yellow football shoes that some yachtsman had traded him. He told us that even though they hurt his feet, he needed them for lobster fishing on the reef because once while stepping on a lobster barefooted he had been bitten. The one night we went lobstering with him he forgot to put them on — he had left them in the canoe in the excitement.

Ituri's immediate neighbors were as big clothes hoarders as he. On one side of him was an old man, who showed us huge chests of clothing. He was looked upon as the rich old man of the island. He was a carver of canoes, bowls, and stone-adze handles, and had been in the yacht-barter business for years. In his chests were suits from all parts of the world. It was strange to run across Brooks Brothers and De Pinna labels in such a place—and such an enormous assortment of sizes piled up in one wardrobe. The old man, fully 75 years of age, was a kind of clothes broker. He never wore anything but a loin cloth himself, but he paid everyone on the island with clothing. When he needed a load of special wood for carving, he paid with a suit. For supplies of fruits and fish, which he was too feeble to go after himself, he paid in the same currency. Every islander liked the idea of owning a complete coat-pants-and-vest suit for Sunday church, and the old man's hut functioned as outfitting headquarters for the island.

Another of Ituri's neighbors was Marii, tall, well built, and as handsome a South Sea islander as one could find. Marii was in his early twenties and married to a typically heavy native woman, who had borne him several children. Marii functioned as native deputy sheriff of Bora Bora —*motoi* is the Tahitian word for his office. He owned a best and a second-best French police cap which, with a khaki tunic, was his uniform. He had few duties, and his official outfit was worn only on movie evenings or to assist the French *préfet* on schooner day. Then he would stand around and look fairly official—in spite of habitually bare feet.

Marii's duties and pay were so slight he fished, made copra, and bartered for clothes as did the rest of the citizenry. Like Ituri, he went in for novelties. The walls of his house were hung with sporting, military, and naval odds and ends which had caught his eye when French and British cruisers visited the island. A British cruiser had paid a sightseeing call on Bora Bora the year preceding our visit. Marii had promptly swapped his wife's supply of grass skirts for a supply of old hats and cast-off bits of uniform. A yellow-and-white-checkered rugby jersey was high on his list of acquisitions. A moth-eaten parade jacket of the British Royal Marines was his pride and joy. He never had nerve enough to flaunt his costumes through the village, but often at home he slipped on various items for only his wife to admire.

One noonday, Marii and Ituri came aboard to take us on a conducted tour of Tupua. Arriving just as Harry and I were doing lunch dishes, they were greatly shocked upon peering down the companionway to see Hazel lying upon a bunk calmly reading a book. In port, Hazel prepared and cooked the food and the male crew took charge of the dishes. Loudly enough for Hazel to hear, I hastily explained matters.

"*Vahine* no good. She sleep, we work."

"*Aite maitai*" (no fine), in chorus.

"How is *your* woman?" I said, turning to Ituri. "She wash your dishes?"

"My woman good. She do all things. Make plenty *hulas* [skirts], make everything my house. My *vahine*, ah, good (with a broad grin). Your *vahine* no good."

"That's right. "*Aite maitai.*"

We departed, leaving Hazel pretty hopping mad at the aspersions. We never did hear the end of it.

It took only a few minutes to sail Ituri's outrigger from our anchorage to Tupua's shore. We were met by an old man who helped beach our canoe and insisted we visit his house, which sat isolated out in the water. It was a small, single-room, thatched house on coconut piling. A pair of cat-walks led from it, one to a little thatched privy and one to a thatched pig pen.

The old man had two grandsons, of whom he was particularly proud. The youngsters were experts at juggling. They had mastered the art of keeping half a dozen oranges in the air at once and performed for us without a fumble. Just as we were ready to leave, I made the mistake of lighting one of our standard kitchen matches on the seat of my pants. To the jugglers as well as the old man, this seemed a feat of magic. Thereupon followed an orgy of match striking which did not cease until several boxes of Ohio Blue Tips which Harry and I had in our pockets were used up. Chinese safety matches (which may be struck only on the box) had been standard Polynesian fire-making equipment for years. Our old-fashioned kitchen matches were a spectacular novelty, and before we left the island we were to have hundreds of requests for the "magic sticks."

The nicest thing about Tupua, we thought, was the view it afforded of Bora Bora. We picked our hats full of wild oranges and climbed to Tupua's summit, about 400 feet up, to feast our eyes upon the lovely peaks across the bay. We had become very fond of native oranges in the course of our voyage. They are not the seedless orange-colored oranges for which California is famous. Island oranges contain large seeds and look greenish yellow or greenish brown when ripe. Once in a while one finds a yellow orange, but this coloration has nothing to do with ripeness. The oranges are ripe when a trifle soft. Ripe ones are very juicy and have a fine, slightly tart flavor. They are rarely eaten by being peeled and broken apart. The usual procedure is to slice off the outer skin with a knife, then bore a hole through the top and suck the juice while squeezing. We picked some oranges which were as big as any we had ever seen. We would have lined up a supply for sailing date but were disappointed to learn that neither Tupua nor Bora Bora has many orange trees or more than enough oranges to go around.

On the way back to the canoe we took a detour into the deep bush and visited "La Cloche," an outjutting of volcanic stone which rings like a bell when struck. It is supposed to have been used in olden times to call worshippers to a heathen temple that once existed nearby.

A bit of excitement came to Bora Bora about the end of our second week at anchor. A little sail was sighted off the north shore and the cry *"Tero, Tero"* was sounded and relayed from house to house until it reached our ears. *"Tero,"* meaning "I see a ship," is supposed to have been derived in early days from the English "sail ho." It is pronounced with the last syllable well drawn out and does, as a matter of fact, sound like "sail ho!" when heard from a distance. Every native takes pride in being first to give the alarm when a speck of sail appears on the horizon. The news travels rapidly by grapevine, or what the French call the "coconut radio," and in a matter of minutes everyone on the island knows what's going on.

This particular *"Tero"* had everyone baffled, because all sail comes to Bora Bora from south and east, as we had done. The only land to the north is Tubai, ten miles away, a small atoll possessing no craft for communication. Tubai is a ring of fringing reef made up of two facing horseshoe-shaped motus, which enclose a lagoon. Copra is made there from several thousand coconut trees, and every three months a special schooner calls to collect it and leave supplies. A French family, the Robesons, are in charge and they hire a dozen natives to work the plantation. The little sail turned out to be a tiny outrigger canoe manned by Mr. Robeson himself and a native. The canoe was like the rest we had seen, designed for protected lagoon sailing, and decidedly out of its element in the heavy ocean swells.

The schooner due at Tubai two months before had failed to put in an appearance, and the Robesons were in the fifth month of isolation. Their cook was out of sugar, flour, canned butter, and beef, and the copra hands were yelling for tobacco. They were sick of fish and coconut sauce and felt they couldn't stand another month of suspense (or longer if their regular schooner were out of commission in Papeete). It was better, Mr. Robeson thought, to risk his life than to wait longer. They had carried Tubai's lone sailing canoe from the lagoon to the outer reef and put to sea, making Bora Bora across the trade wind in six hours. Only constant bailing and alert handling under shortened sail had saved them from foundering en route. Mr. Robeson's mission was well-timed. Bora Bora's monthly trading schooner, the old Chinese-

owned *Denise,* appeared the day following his spectacular arrival. The captain of the *Denise* consented to put in at Tubai, and the Robeson canoe was swung onto its deck for his return trip.

We couldn't resist Mr. Robeson's invitation to visit his domain. We told Marii to keep an eye on *Viator,* watching that our anchors didn't drag, and boarded the *Denise* for Tubai. We were just a day on Tubai, and it was a day of most lavish and unexpected hospitality. The *Denise* anchored off the reef and we went ashore by long boat, passing through a cut in the outer coral just large enough to float us when the surge of the sea was right. Here the skill of the man at the steering sweep, and the alert power of the two stalwarts on the oars synchronized so smoothly that the very difficult feat of seamanship looked almost easy.

Mrs. Robeson, flanked by 14 of her 17 children and the native help, welcomed us and led us through the coconut trees to her home on the edge of the great lagoon. As soon as the long-desired supplies arrived in her kitchen, a feast was gotten under way that surpassed anything we had yet seen for abundance. The captain of the *Denise*, Hazel, Harry, Mr. Robeson and I were served by a great force of children and natives led by Mrs. Robeson, who couldn't have flitted about more gaily if we had been a party of celebrities. After lunch we found out a bit about Mrs. Robeson but not before she had questioned us at length concerning our cruise of the islands in Harry's boat, and remarked with much French volubility upon Hazel's courage to sail in such a small craft. Mrs. Robeson had not been off the atoll in 22 years. She had accompanied her husband to his post as a bride and borne him 17 children, the three eldest of whom were in school in Papeete. All had been delivered without benefit of doctor or midwife. And she thought small-boat sailing was risky!

Her love for the life she led was pronounced and genuine. Only the problem of educating her children would eventually cause her to take up residence in Papeete. For the present, an older daughter, returned from Papeete schooling, leads the younger children in religious education and teaches them the rudiments of grammar, spelling, and arithmetic. We visited the open-air classroom and saw the same evidences of careful training we had observed at the serving of the meal. We couldn't help but think of the whining, restless children in some American families of our acquaintance. Here were youngsters with no toys, radios, movies, nor television—dependent upon one another for every diversion and stimulation—yet with as composed and contented miens as one could imagine. In Papeete they will no doubt receive certain beneficial book learning which has been denied them on Tubai. They will also make new friends and find broader horizons. On the other hand, their happy ignorance of the world of *things* will cease. They will suddenly learn of *things* and need *things* the rest of their lives. Only after years of struggle will they look back upon childhood and appreciate, as we appreciated, the priceless simplicity of their life.

We can thank Mrs. Robeson for imparting to us a very earthy legend. Most legends we had heard dealt either with lovers who were turned into stone or with ancient warriors endowed with supernatural strength. Mrs. Robeson's legend was different—it had a semimodern angle:

Several hundred years ago two white seamen, half dead from exposure and thirst, drifted upon the outer reef of Tubai. They were carried ashore by natives almost simultaneously with the falling apart of the rotten little ship's boat which had brought them thither. Where they came from was not recorded; we can surmise that they were deserters from the round-the-world cruise of Magellan, who passed through the western Pacific in 1521. Or they may have been obstreperous seamen set adrift from one of the ships of Mendaña's fleet, which in 1594 discovered the Marquesas in the name of the wife of the Viceroy of Peru. Whoever they were, upon being nursed to health they became great favorites on Tubai and everyone in the community looked upon them as gods.

Tubai at this period was a dependency of Bora Bora. It was Bora Bora's fishing preserve, and it contained a large sacrificial *marae* visited upon occasion by warriors and priests of the governing island. The group of resident natives on Tubai was small, their lives monotonous. They functioned as caretakers, with nothing much to do between visits of their lords and masters. Therefore the company of the white men was important to them and they resolved to insure its permanency.

They invented a cunning lie. In vivid sign language they made it clear that if the presence of the whites became known on Bora Bora, the two sailors would be killed. They would either be taken away and clubbed to death before the eyes of Bora Bora's king, or be killed on Tubai and their bones thrown upon the *marae* with the rest of the victims of sacrifice. In terror, the sailors agreed to keep out of sight. They spent their time in a little shelter hidden deep in jungle growth on the rarely visited eastern side of the atoll. Food was brought to them regularly, and at intervals committees of Tubaians called to pay them homage. But once strong and well again, the sailors grew restless. They took to prowling in the dead of night, timing their walks so as to be back in their retreat well before dawn.

On one of these walks they were startled by sounds of soft, rippling laughter and the splash and gurgle of water. The sounds came from the dense growth inland and were clear and distinct above the low boom of surf on the reef. Investigating, they discovered a clearing in the bush not 500 yards away—in a place that had been impenetrable the night before! Peering cautiously from a circle of bordering coconut trees, they beheld a sight that froze them in their tracks.

In the center of the clearing was an oval pool surrounded by low, heavily flowered *tiare* bushes. Half drugged by incense from the myriad blooms, they fancied themselves mad as they gazed into the pool and beheld two of the most divinely formed nymphs ever seen by man, scooping silvery water with dippers of polished coconut shell. The nymphs poured the contents first over one dark shoulder and then the other, and the waters found their way back to the pool via curves indescribable.

For several nights the white men were content merely to gaze and admire—patient Peeping Toms, too overcome to make their presence known, and fearful lest the exquisite tableau dissolve at the slightest sound. Each night they returned to their abode with the trembling resolve that the following night they would test the mirage qualities of what they had seen. Daylight hours were spent wishing for darkness.

The night finally came when they could keep their peace no longer. They confronted the beauteous nymphs and to their surprise found them to be both alive and receptive. Hours of starlight sped by as split seconds, yet not too quickly for each sailor to realize he had found the great love of his life. Let the dawn come, let the alarm go to Bora Bora, nothing mattered now!

But dawn turned the tables. The first rays of the sun revealed faces enmeshed in a thousand wrinkles and two forms hideous with the sag of aged flesh. The sailors looked into the eyes of two deformed hags. The pool was dried up and the *tiare* bushes were flowerless. So great was the shock of disillusionment (these were sensitive sailors) they ran out to the reef and jumped into the sea, to be eaten by the sharks.

Mrs. Robeson told the tale with great charm and almost shed a tear at the climax. She said the Deities' Bath was still to be seen on moonless nights, and once in a while, when the wind was right, the soft ripple of laughter had been known to float clear across the lagoon and into her bedroom window.

This tale being one of those things to torment the imagination, we had cause for wonder months later as we browsed among the pages of *Cook's Voyages,* and read the following:

> On the 24th (November 1777, at anchor in Raiatea) I was informed that a midshipman and a seaman both belonging to the *Discovery* were missing. As the midshipman was known to have expressed a desire to remain at these islands, it seemed pretty certain that he and his companion had gone off with this intention and Captain Clerke set out in quest of them with two armed boats and a party of marines. The expedition proved fruitless and Captain Clerke seemed to think that the natives intended to conceal the deserters and with that view had amused themselves with false information the whole day and directed him to search for them in places where they were not to be found.
> The Captain judged right for the next morning we were told that our runaways were at Tahaa. As these two were not the only persons in the ship who wished to end their days at these favourite islands, in order to put a stop to any further desertion, it was necessary to get them back at all events.

With this resolve, Cook went into action. He immediately seized the son, daughter and son-in-law of Chief Oreo as hostages and ordered Oreo to produce the deserters forthwith. Within four days the men were captured on Tubai and returned by sailing canoe to Cook's command. Cook's words sum up the episode:

> They had reached Tahaa the same night they deserted, but finding it impossible to go to any of the islands to the eastward for want of wind, they had proceeded to Bora Bora and from thence to the small island Tubai, where they were taken. As soon as they were delivered on board, the three hostages were released. Thus ended an affair which had given me much trouble and vexation. Nor would I have exerted myself so resolutely to the occasion but for the reason mentioned, and to save the son of a brother officer from being lost to his country.

The return trip of the *Denise* to Bora Bora was one continuous picnic. The Robesons loaded us with things to eat until we began to fear that Mr. Robeson would have to sail again for supplies before we were out of sight. A young native couple leaving Tubai for a Papeete holiday, their first in three years, played a guitar and sang, and we divided the few hours' passage listening to them and talking with the half-caste supercargo. Through the supercargo we heard more about the sinking of the *Vahioti,* a schooner which went down in Raiatea's lagoon a few years previous under such peculiar circumstances "the sinking of the *Vahioti*" was still a table topic through the islands.

The *Vahioti* incident was the climax to a series of schooner mishaps which had had all the insurance companies guessing for a decade. Schooners were foundering, especially in the Tuamotus, with such regularity that underwriters couldn't adjust their rates fast enough to keep pace. They suspected foul play but had no proof.

As the story goes, "the 150-ton schooner *Vahioti* sailed from Huahine, Raiatea-bound, upon as beautiful an August day as the South Seas have ever produced." Besides some native passengers and 35 pigs, she carried "three expensive motor trucks and a hold full of sugar, gasoline, and kerosene." Just 5 miles from Raiatea, passengers noticed the captain and mate engaged in a heated argument, but assumed some triviality had annoyed the old man, a well-known and rather eccentric skipper. An hour later the *Vahioti* lowered sail, started her motor, and came slowly through Raiatea's pass. Just as she was about to turn and swing toward the jetty, she stopped dead; watchers on shore saw her decks become suddenly alive with excitement and life boats being lowered. Before they could comprehend what was taking place, the *Vahioti* sank to the bottom in five fathoms, her masts and rigging towering strangely from the smooth green top of the lagoon.

Salvaging the cargo of the *Vahioti* was the simplest job ever tackled by the native divers. The protected lagoon and easy depth made for quick work. Within ten minutes after salvaging started, it was discovered that the oil cans aboard the vessel were filled with salt water instead of oil, and sugar sacks with sand; the motor trucks so carefully wrapped and padded against damage were motorless dummies, and only the pigs, two-thirds of which had drowned, were genuine. As for the fast sinking, a section of planking large enough for one to put head and shoulders through had been knocked out just below the waterline.

This explained the argument between captain and mate. They had been ordered to sink the ship at sea halfway between Huahine and Raiatea. They could there take to the boats and row with the wind to safety—or, if they didn't care to row they could easily drift to Raiatea. But at the critical moment the mate had sought to hide his fright in argument. By the time he recovered nerve enough to start the *Vahioti's* bung, she was halfway in the pass.

Back in Bora Bora, we spruced up *Viator* and opened our charts for the run westward to Maupiti. It would be short—27 miles from pass to pass—but round-the-world yachtsman, William A. Robinson's, account* of the Maupiti pass had us worried. We reread a few pages of his book and found certain lines far from reassuring:

> "Few boats ever enter Maupiti's lone pass, which is very narrow and dangerous.... With the breeze at all south to southeast it is impossible.... A strong current pours out of the narrow, tortuous channel and meets the incoming swell, forming treacherous seas and boilers in the very pass itself...."

We talked to Bora Bora's *préfet,* to the school teacher, and to the captain of the *Denise* in an effort to get local knowledge about the dangers ahead, but none had been in Maupiti's pass. Nor did we find a native on Bora Bora who had even been to Maupiti—a curious condition, but typical of many island communities. Apparently only strangers fraternize throughout the group. When natives leave the island of their birth they usually visit Papeete, the metropolis. Interisland hobnobbing is almost as restricted as it was in ancient warlike times.

Ituri and Marii were most apologetic for their lack of information and hastily offered us some seafaring logic based upon their limited observations after years of local reef fishing. They contended that all we need consider was the three-day surf cycle. For three days the surf is high, then for three days the surf is low. It must, they claimed, follow the same routine at Maupiti that it always had done at Bora Bora, excluding of course, periods of storm.

They pointed toward the pass and showed us we were in a cycle of high surf. The spray had been dashing wildly for 24 hours. In two more days the low cycle would arrive and then we should sail for Maupiti—not before. In addition, we could take advantage of the daily cycle. Early each morning the seas are lowest. Noon they are at their worst. If we sailed away from Bora Bora at midnight two days hence, we would arrive at Maupiti for the dawn surf of the easy cycle.

Two afternoons later we took up our anchors and moved to the dock lately occupied by the *Denise.* We carefully filled the water tanks from Bora Bora's plentiful supply, realizing no surplus water would be avail-

---

Ten Thousand Leagues Over the Sea.

able on either Maupiti or Mopelia and our 120 gallons would have to last to Rarotonga, many weeks and many hundreds of miles away. By 7:00 p.m. we had shaken hands with our friends, completed an exchange of gifts, again giving *Viator* the aspect of a market cart, set our alarm clock for midnight, and turned in.

We all slept on deck—Harry in the cockpit, Hazel and I on the cabin trunk—and the midnight alarm found us greatly refreshed and eager to be off. All was black and quiet as a tomb. The stars were so obscured by low-hanging clouds, the sky above Bora Bora's monster silhouette was just a shade less black than the silhouette itself. We were sure of one thing: If we proceeded NNE across the bay we would in a few hundred yards see two range beacons which Marii promised to place on the shore north above his house. These would guide us out through the pass. By keeping them in a line over our stern we would find the center of the channel, with nothing to impede our progress to deep water.

As we turned on the motor and loosed our lines, a single light pierced the darkness. It was from a lantern carried by a small boy who had come to try his luck fly-fishing on the reflecting surface off the dock piling. We stopped a few minutes to watch as he flitted the hook, camouflaged in frayed string, back and forth by our stern. His lantern attracted countless fish to the surface and he landed two little ones before we churned away.

Hazel sat at the tiller with eyes glued to the compass, and Harry and I hung on the jib stay, searching the black velvet off the starboard quarter for beacons. One hundred yards, two hundred yards, three hundred yards—and no beacons. We slowed down the motor as far as it would go without danger of dying and took a guess at our position— then turned more toward where the pass should be. Still no lights on the island, excepting the boy's lantern back on the dock. It was just a pin prick in the blackness.

On the reef now several torches could be distinguished. Natives after lobster. Perhaps that widest gap between the torches was the pass? We edged closer to it and the lights shifted, making a gap half a mile away suddenly appear to be the widest. There was the chance that we might duplicate the deed of the middle-of-the-road pedestrian who figured the lights of an approaching cross-country bus were two motorcycles. Nothing to do but cautiously motor back to the dock—about-face and slowly cover the reverse of our course.

But where is the boy's lantern? That lantern is our most valuable landmark at the moment. There it is—isn't that it flickering faintly over there? Yes, it seems to be, but what if the boy has moved and is fishing from a coral head close to the shore? During an hour of very heavy suspense we vainly tried to locate the dock. The boy's lamp was like a firefly (we found later he had carried it to the village and back twice during our ordeal), and the more we watched it the more we agreed it would be disastrous to depend upon it. Our apprehension was not for ourselves—no physical calamity could overtake us in the smooth and protected lagoon. The great anxiety was for the boat. Every minute for what seemed like hours we feared *Viator* would run up on coral and gouge planking from her bottom. We were as lost as a blind-flying plane whose instruments and radio have gone out of commission. At length we cut our motor off entirely and tried calling, in hopes the boy and lantern would come to the dock's end and stay put. We watched and waited. The lantern appeared to be stationary at last. We crept closer and were finally in. The boy had heard our calls.

Never was a man so embarrassed as was Marii when we tumbled him from his bed and marched him down the beach. In his confusion he forgot to put on either his best or second-best police hat, and clad only in a pair of blue polka-dot shorts he looked far from official as he banged on the bamboo walls of the beacon keeper's hut. The rusty coal-oil lanterns had been taken down after the *Denise* sailed, and Marii's orders to hang them out for us had slipped the keeper's mind.

The Eighth Island—MAUPITI

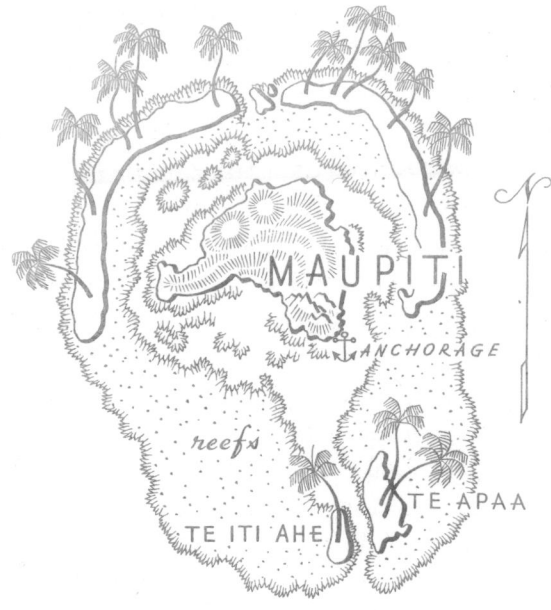

F ALSE starts are supposed to be bad luck for sailors, but the run to
Maupiti was uneventful. Our delay with the beacons, however,
was no help so far as keeping our schedule was concerned. Because of
the delay we didn't arrive off Maupiti's pass until high noon—just when
the current was supposed to be behaving its worst. Instead, a peaceful
scene confronted us. The pass and passage, guarded at the entrance by
the islets Te Iti Ahe and Te Apaa, stretched away to the castlelike cliffs
more like a great green strip of waxed linoleum than two miles of dangerous, current-swept channel. The surf was breaking pretty high on
each side of the outer entrance, but the narrow opening was inviting
enough, and several natives waved to us from canoes a hundred yards
inside.

As we took off sail and turned on the motor, one of the canoes
paddled confidently out the pass and came alongside. In it was Fano,
a tall, European-looking Maupitian who turned out to be the only in-
habitant of the island who spoke anything but Tahitian. His English
was the best we had encountered thus far. He had worked for ten years
as able seaman on ships America- and Australia-bound from Tahiti.
We took him aboard, his canoe in tow, and as we threaded our way up
the channel, canoe after canoe joined our procession until we had a

serpentine of a dozen towing behind us. All the canoes were loaded down with fish, and amidst much laughing and yelling many were held up and shown to us. Some small red ones were eaten raw as we watched, heads and all. Everyone seemed in a holiday mood and glad to see us.

There must be some confusion in the U.S. Hydrographic Bureau concerning the size of Maupiti. The *Pilot Book* says the island is six miles long and, together with the islet-studded reef, covers an area 20 miles in circumference. The latest government chart (No. 2023) showed the island to be a mile and a quarter long and, with the surrounding reef, nine miles in total circumference! Whatever the circumference, the main feature, the "rocky bluff, 700 feet high, which resembles a castle," dominates the whole scene, and once ashore we managed to walk around it via a little path along the water in less than three hours. Our walk was leisurely. Fano had us in tow and stopped at practically every house to introduce us around and point out his relations.

To the old schooner captain who is reported to have said, "All South Sea islands are the same—see one and you have seen them all," a visit to Maupiti is recommended. At every turn we were to discover something new and different. First of all, we were surprised to note the island had no village such as we had been accustomed to finding. Some thatched huts were clustered on shore by our anchorage, but they were merely a concentration of the string of dwellings which dot the shore all the way around.

Four hundred and twenty is the population of Maupiti—all native with the exception of a lone Chinaman who runs Maupiti's single dinky store. There hadn't been a French official in residence for years. Rule is vested in a chief who, backed up by the deacons of the church, has everything to say. Every last one of the 420 inhabitants is a member of the church and, with the exception of the newly born and aged-infirm, takes active part in its devotions. The creed is basically Protestant, having been planted a century ago by London Missionary Society people before the island came under French rule. It is doubtful, however, that the church practices left by the old missionaries continued for long in their original form.

The big church activity today centers in the *himine* house, a large, oval, bamboo structure with a mat-covered dirt floor. Our first night at anchor we were invited to attend, and found it highly interesting. A goodly 150 of the congregation turned out. The rest, Fano hastened to explain, would attend the next affair a few days hence. Even so, more natives were on hand than the edifice could accommodate. There were quite as many people seated on the ground outside as inside.

When we entered and found places on a mat at the rear of the room, everyone nodded and smiled. At the head of the room, facing the audience, a native in a black suit sat on the only seat in the place. He leaned upon a table which supported his Bible and the only source of illumination, a coal-oil lamp. He was the preacher, but functioned more as chairman of the meeting. The speaking was all done by men, and after each speech was ended, singing, dominated by female voices and remindful of the Huahine wake, split our eardrums. Fano did his best to interpret what went on—the talks were all biblical anecdotes, he said, sometimes interwoven with local legendary material.

Some horseplay occurred, too. One fellow who talked overtime was pinched from behind by a couple of his snickering brethren until he had to turn around and admonish them. As he paused to do so, someone started the singing and he was forced to sit down in disgust, much to everyone's amusement. There was no visible leader of the singing. It started automatically and simultaneously with whoever uttered the first note. Another fellow who tried to speak a second time was so severely squelched, we pitied him. He was quite fancily dressed in a brass-buttoned naval jacket and white flannels, which made his embarrassment all the more pathetic. Each time he scrambled to his feet after a song and addressed the chair with the customary "iorana," the song would start again and he would stand for a while nervously wriggling his toes before squatting in resignation. He tried half a dozen times before he gave up. It reminded us of a hackneyed vaudeville gag in which the orchestra keeps breaking into repeat choruses of Sousa's *Lights Out March* as the comedian clears his throat to sing.

Finally one very long ballad was sung in which everyone was quite serious. It was the story of a Maupiti Timi, with biblical allusions thrown in. This Timi was one of the island's favorite sons. The seventeen-year-old Timi had been stevedoring copra in Papeete. One day he sailed away from Tahiti on a little boat and died in a far-off land, and his soul was received in Heaven. That was the gist of the song as explained to us.

Fano wasn't aware that we already knew something of the story of Timi and thus this demonstration was every bit as moving to us as it was to all at the *himine*. Timi had sailed from Papeete on a little American ketch. It was the *Idle Hour*, owned by Dwight Long, a young man from Seattle, Washington. Long had undergone much the same crew experience in Papeete as had Harry. He had signed on Timi as a substitute crew and set out for Samoa and around the world.* When the *Idle Hour* was two weeks from Australia the enthusiastic Timi contracted pneumonia and three days after they tied up at Sydney he was dead.

After the *himine*, Fano guided us to the house of Timi's people and showed us a clipping that had been mailed to them from Australia. It was from a Sydney paper and carried a picture of Timi's grave.

Everyday life on Maupiti was the most active of any island we had visited thus far. On other islands, we had caught only occasional glimpses of men in loincloth bringing in the breadfruit, and bare-breasted women grating coconut, while bedsteads, bicycles, and movies never lost their importance. The people of Maupiti, disdaining bedsteads, bicycles, and movies, were different. Here, loinclothed men and bare-breasted women were the rule, rather than the exception.

We were struck immediately by the evidences of native industry on all sides. Every household was busily engaged in something. Women sat upon the porches weaving mats and hats of pandanus. Old men braided rope of coconut fiber and *purau*. Young men swung along the paths with poles upon their shoulders, balancing double loads of taro root, papaya, and breadfruit. Three canoes were in course of construction within sight of our boat, and the steady chink of adzes filled the air with a rhythmic sound that gave the days a certain tempo. Each household, too, exhibited some stage in the preparation of manioca — a staple food of the island which, when served, is a gelatinous dish similar to tapioca. We saw great areas of growing manioca and noticed that some of the front yards displayed enormous trays of the extracted white powder drying in the sun. In answer to our question regarding the apparent surplus of hats, mats, cordage, and manioca, Fano explained that much of it was sent to Papeete for marketing. "But no boats

Dwight Long sailed more than 50,000 miles to complete his voyage around the world from Seattle to Seattle on Idle Hour. *Then he returned to Tahiti to film a lovely documentary movie on island life, "Tanga Tika," which, as this is written, is having its premier showing in the United States.*

ever call at Maupiti," we countered. "How does the stuff reach its destination?"

Fano answered this with information which was news to us. "My father," he said, "whom you will meet in a few days, has run a schooner from Maupiti to Tahiti as long as I can remember. It should not even be called a schooner. It is an old tub of a thing. It leaks so much the pumping never stops. It is half again as long as your *Viator* but everything about it is worn out. The sails are so old and patched they rip in the wind. Something breaks every time it goes to sea. It has no engine and sometimes it lies outside our pass for days until the wind is just right to come in. Sometimes when there is no wind we go out to the reef and pull it through with ropes. Six weeks ago my father took it to Tahiti loaded with copra. On deck were twenty-five of our people and eleven pigs. They carried coconuts and manioca for food and drink but they did not carry enough. I know that some of the pigs died before they got to Tahiti, and were thrown overboard. I know how bad it was because I used to sail with my father."

Fano and his father had operated on a partnership basis, but the old man had taken to spending their profits on the night life of Papeete. When Fano objected, he was reminded that the ship was the property of the father. Fano thereafter remained upon Maupiti and the boat was pumped and manned by passengers. Fano worried greatly that one day the craft would sail for Tahiti and not be heard of again.

"It was no good when my father bought it forty years ago from a Papeete junk yard," he said. "When the mast bends to port, every seam on the starboard side opens up. On the other tack all the planks to port separate and let the ocean in."

This kind of navigating didn't dovetail very well with the dangerous reputation of Maupiti's pass, and we questioned Fano on the subject.

"The pass is rarely too bad for us," he said. "Of course, when the hurricane roars, we do not try to go through."

"Has any ship ever been lost there? Was anyone ever killed?"

"Only once. Maybe twenty years ago. We had another schooner then, the *Tatoi,* and she tried to come in when the wind was very strong from the south. She was broken to pieces on the reef and everyone was drowned while we watched. There were ten men, six girls, and two little babies. Only two bodies were found—two of the girls. I myself found them a week later way around the reef to the west. Their eyes were eaten out by the little fish. The sea threw them on the reef and saved them from the sharks."

There was but one other incident in Fano's memory in connection with the pass. A half dozen years before, a small American ketch, the *Fayaway*, had paid them a visit. Her crew had inquired, as we had, about the pass, and determined deliberately to shoot out to sea when it was at its worst. It seems the skipper of the *Fayaway* was writing a book. He did, however, heed Fano in certain particulars. He lashed himself to the wheel and put his two companions below, under battened hatches, before speeding up the motor and heading out.

As a crowd of Maupitians stood on Te Iti Ahe and watched, the *Fayaway* plunged into the inrushing swell like a hell-diver. Three times she went so far out of sight that only a bit of the rigging was visible above the foam, but each time she shook her way to the surface and carried on. The boys were so jubilant when they were at last clear of the rollers, they stood in the cockpit and gave three lusty cheers for Maupiti. They hoisted sail and stood off to sea, happy that they had taunted the disaster gods and won. They were undismayed by the fact that every movable article had been washed clear of the deck. Coconuts, bananas, even their lifeboat had disappeared in the terrific buffeting.

Fano shook his head in disgust as he rolled some stringy-looking tobacco in a strip of pandanus. "They were crazy," he said. "And very lucky. I hope you don't try anything like that."

Never again will we enjoy such swimming facilities as were offered by Maupiti's lagoon. A short paddle from our boat, a white sand bar, extending toward us from the fringing reef, furnished the private beach of our dreams. Each morning and evening Hazel and I used it, sharing our seclusion only with a group of tiny hermit crabs who drew into their shells upon our approach and stayed there. The deep water was so clear we could almost count the grains of bottom sand, and the shallow water so transparent it was impossible to detect where water and beach joined.

Some days, when we tired of our perfect swimming pool, we paddled farther along to a coral garden abounding in fish that outrivaled for coloring those we had seen in Tahiti. Besides large, gaudily decorated creatures emblazoned with faces of circus clowns, there were minute fish so brilliant they seemed illuminated from within. Certain pieces of coral proved to be the habitual rendezvous of certain tiny fish and drew us again and again to stare in wonder. One particularly heroic piece of stag's horn coral never failed to thrill us as we thrust our diving glasses close to its contours. A few inches from its crevices hundreds of small blue fish hung motionlessly suspended. They were the unreal blue of tropical butterfly wings. They looked as though they might easily be scooped up with the hand, but at any sudden movement or at the approach of a normal-sized, prowling fish, they would disappear in a lightninglike flash which the eye could not follow. It was like the reaction of bits of steel filing to the sudden impulse of a giant electro-magnet.

As for the larger fish, one can understand the difficulties confronting artists commissioned by museums to reproduce their variegated designs for publication. The fish may not be brought to the surface, because their tinctures fade to gray on contact with the atmosphere. All study must be done through waterglasses, making it impossible to approach close enough for absolute accuracy. Even in our superficial gazing we were confused by the chameleonlike qualities of what we saw. We found many examples where coloring was only apparent—where closer scrutiny revealed hues unnoticed from a distance. For instance, a particular fish appeared to carry a bright orange triangle below its first dorsal fin. Closer inspection showed the triangle to be a yellow area filled with red polka dots. Then a still closer look revealed both the dots and the background as myriad designs within designs embodying more variations of color.

Maupiti was famed for one lagoon fish, the *eihe* (pronounced eehyee, with a grunt in the middle). The *eihe* started to run a few days after we arrived, and one night, while Hazel and Harry were entertaining some of the village elders aboard *Viator,* I took our largest Coleman gasoline lantern and embarked with Fano and a couple of his young nephews to join the chase. Our canoe, with one of the youngsters straddling the bow and holding the light, edged out into the darkness, and a dozen others followed, making a torchlight procession half a mile long.

Our white light was really a jarring note in the picture, but Fano was quite proud of it because it required no attention, and he knew we were exciting the envy of the others, who burned bunches of dry palm fronds which had to be constantly replaced. The palm fronds, wrapped in bundles six feet long and as big around as a man, protruded from the canoes like flaming bowsprits and set up a great crackling and spitting which one would have imagined equal to frightening every fish from the lagoon. At times, too, great burning segments fell into the water to become extinguished after loud sputtering and fizzing. But noise didn't seem to worry the *eihes* in the slightest.

Before we had proceeded halfway across the lagoon, *eihes* were jumping all around us, a few in their enthusiasm even flipping into our canoe of their own accord. They looked like midget swordfish, about eight inches long and half an inch thick, and were the hand-painted color of the large mounted specimens one sees in museums.

Fano stood with a foot on either gunwale and wielded his big six-pronged spear on the same principle by which gardeners stab at dry leaves. Some he captured in midair, as far off as the outrigger, and many times he snared half a dozen before he was content to pause and extricate his catch.

I didn't do too well, I must admit. For the first half hour I had Fano's nephews in stitches as I lunged to one side then the other, slicing the water always an instant after the quarry had moved out of range. At moments I was sure I was the object of a conspiracy hatched between the natives and the *eihes*. It seemed incredible I could miss such closely packed targets. Then, just as we were ready to turn around for home, I began to get the knack of the thing. I found I could sufficiently antici-pate the antics of the *eihes* to capture every tenth one I tried for.

All the canoes returned to the beach loaded with the tiny fish, and every family lugged off a basket or two. We had a frying panful for breakfast next day, and they were excellent.

One afternoon the ship of Fano's father sailed into the lagoon and tied up against a bit of dock not far from us. The boat was everything Fano had claimed for it. So worn and blistered was the ancient coat of paint, our own craft looked like a new toy in comparison. Paint had been applied to the transom so many times without the preliminary scraping away of old layers that the letters of many names showed through in indecipherable confusion. The boat had been renamed so often in seventy-five years it had no name. Fano was right about the pumping, too. Not until all sail was down and the old planking had a chance to press together again at the seams, free from the pull of bending masts, was the creaking pump abandoned. The passengers had taken turns pumping all the way—men and women alike.

We stood on the dock with Fano and met the newcomers as they stepped ashore. They were very gay and seemed not much the worse for wear. All the women carried bundles tied in *pareu* cloth—bundles containing spare clothing and left-over food they had stocked up with in Papeete. Each also carried a large black umbrella, the only protection against sun and rain en route. Two extra passengers added to the excitement. A handsome young woman and her five-year-old son had stayed in Tahiti from the last trip and now were returning. The boy was as white-skinned and blond as the mother was bronzed and black-haired.

"Ah, those boys liked our girls very much," explained Fano. "Someday that skipper will come back and see what he left behind him." Fano had not before mentioned this aspect of the *Fayaway's* visit.

Fano's father, struggling with a crate of chickens, greeted us with a smile. "Maybe big *hula* tonight," he said, dropping the chickens and shaking our hands. He was a fine-looking fellow, about sixty, gray-headed and wearing a little mustache. Rather heavy pouches under his eyes intimated that the trip had been a personal success. He had the light olive·skin and Polynesian features found in pictures of the aristocracy of another generation, but in stature he was rather diminutive. The top of his head came up just about to Fano's shoulder. But his ideas for "*hula* tonight" caught on, and it was arranged that we come to Fano's around 7:00 and bring our gasoline lantern.

Besides the lantern, we loaded ourselves with everything we could think of which might contribute to the "*hula*." We arrived with a basket containing four quarts of rum, canned pineapple, cartons of cigarettes, and a jar of maraschino cherries. The rum was the last of our liquor supply, save for one bottle which we thought it best to keep for an emergency. Four quarts were not much, but the islanders, with the exception of Fano's father, were temperate and everyone would get a taste. Again and again, as Fano's wife stirred the rum and fruit in two five-gallon gasoline tins, Fano counseled more water. At last when the concoction was diluted to the brims of both containers, he pronounced it just right. Then we adjourned to the path under the trees and the affair was on.

We were installed upon three chair bottoms (we had seen children scrubbing them earlier in the afternoon in the lagoon), and beside us on the ground sat the orchestra—four young men with battered guitars.

The Coleman lantern was placed in the middle of a circle of about thirty squatting youths all dressed in Sunday finery, and we imagined a troupe of female performers were somewhere off in the shadows adjusting their grass skirts for the dance. For perhaps half an hour we sat while Fano played the perfect host. He walked round and round the circle offering the tins of punch and a dipper, while the orchestra played island tunes and sang softly. We distributed our cigarettes and drank from the dipper with the rest, feeling that any minute Maupiti's beauties would appear. But nothing of the sort happened and at last we questioned Fano.

"Where are the dancing girls? Have we done something to frighten them away?"

"On Maupiti our girls leave the dancing to our men."

The first to dance were a pair of female impersonators, and for an instant we wondered if we were in for some tribal dance that might prove embarrassing. But the dancing was superb. The dancers were truly wonderful to behold. They wore grass skirts over red *pareus,* and each boyish head was crowned with a heavy garland of *tiare.* Around their ankles and wrists were pompons of frayed pandanus, and around their necks were more flower garlands, which swung as they swayed to the primitive tempo furnished by the band. The dance was at once more finished and less vulgar than the usual hula, and everyone in the circle looked on with an attitude of sincere appreciation. After several encores the dancers bowed away into the darkness and a few minutes later reappeared before us with flower crowns for our heads. They had earlier in the evening plaited them as a surprise—huge, ornate crowns with double rows of palm barbs protruding two feet into the air.

Then came the real surprise of the evening. The musicians played a hybrid waltz, and all the young men rose and waltzed together with the flourish of the Victorian era. It all seemed especially incongruous, following as it did right after the hula. We looked in vain for a trace of humor on the faces that danced before us, but everyone was in dead earnest. These young men who fished and worked on the hillside each day excelled in the waltz by night! And they showed the skill of long practice, bare feet gliding over the hard-packed dirt as gracefully as dancing pumps move over smooth hardwood.

But this wasn't all. Hardly were we accustomed to the waltz than the music changed to the time of a French gavotte. Partners were shaking index fingers coyly at each other and breaking into beautifully executed pirouettes in perfect accord with the accompaniment. This was almost too much. Here were the intricate movements one has forever associated with the silk-and-satin courts of Louis XV—presented on a South Sea island path by gaslight. And executed wholly by men! Men in loincloths and polo shirts. Some with loose-fitting, white undershirts and denim shorts.

I turned to Fano for explanation. The ballroom dancing, he said, had come to Maupiti before the memory of anyone on the island. According to Fano's father, it had been introduced at the time of the first missionaries in an attempt to replace the heathen hula. It persisted, not because of any deep-seated native preference but because it was a novelty for special occasions.

"We call it the *acacion,* and I do not know what that word means. Pretty soon it will be over and you will see one of our Maupiti dances."

When the music stopped, four of the dancers went to the center of the ring and put their heads close together, in the manner a radio quartet surrounds a microphone, and began to hum with hands cupped over their mouths. Two had harmonicas and played them with a bass-viol staccato which the others mimicked with their lips.

"Waha waha waha waha, thrum thrum thrum thrum—Waha waha waha waha, thrum thrum thrum thrum" came the time, and a circle of dancers formed. On the "wahas" the line progressed clockwise, as a sort of trotting chain gang. On the "thrums," pairs faced each other and executed the "bumps." The ballroom seriousness was gone. Every face was suddenly lit up as though someone had commanded one and all to register happiness. Had we not seen an hour of decorous waltzing and gavotting after the disappearance of the last drop of punch, one might have thought that the whole thing was the rum speaking.

Round and round they went. Sometimes the beat speeded to such an extent the dancers could scarcely keep up. Then, when the cadence dropped as if to give the quartet a breathing spell, the movements were tripped in slow motion and shadows shifted grotesquely away from the light. All in all, it was exceedingly barbarous, in spite of the blue shorts and polo shirts.

The hit of the evening was not the punch nor the cigarettes nor the cherries, but the canned pineapple. At home we often sip fruit punch and leave the pineapple for someone to throw out; on Maupiti, many a dipperful of punch was spilled to the ground in the search for bits of pineapple. Some fresh pineapple is grown in Tahiti, but the canned article was something new, and when it was gone the cry was "Aite pineappo ua oti" (No pineapple; finished). After the last dance the entire party accompanied us to our canoe and as we paddled out to *Viator*, "Aite pineappo ua oti" was a goodnight chant ringing in our ears as we clambered aboard.

Next day Fano came to the boat carrying a little portable phonograph that someone had left on the island years before. The machine had ceased to play almost simultaneously with the departure of the donor and he had kept it, hoping someone would come along and repair it. In a few minutes Harry had it running as well as our own and Fano was overjoyed. None of us had the heart to tell Fano what was really the matter. The automatic stop had been advanced so that each record clicked to a halt before it got going! Only that had kept it out of commission for years. While Harry took the machine apart to give it a good oiling, I took up Fano's invitation to climb Maupiti's castlelike bluff.

The walk proved much more to my taste than the fast-paced marches I had made with Harry. Fano was as gentle in his gait as he was in his speech. We made frequent stops and consumed a couple of hours before we reached the highest point and sat upon a rocky ledge sheer above the lagoon.

A few sea birds wheeled around us, but otherwise the island was mysteriously lifeless. It was noon and no canoes were on the lagoon. Halfway up we had lost sight of *Viator* and the old schooner. We were viewing a lovely diorama, enjoying an exclusive peek at a South Sea island before the coming of man. Somewhere back to the east, Bora Bora and Tubai lay obscured in a curtain of haze which rested upon the sea like early-morning steam on a mill pond. To the north, south, and west the blue Pacific stretched to seeming eternity. It emphasized our remoteness from everything as no chart could. Maupiti was our jumping-off place, and Mopelia, the small and solitary atoll we were to seek in the west, lay a hundred miles over the far horizon as the trade winds blew.

When Fano became at last convinced that we were bent upon weighing anchor and had but a few days left with him and his Maupitians, he more than redoubled his efforts to amuse and entertain us.

We were taken to the stamping ground of Moho, an ancient cannibal god who left a pair of Gargantuan knee prints on the lava-encrusted windward shore of the island. Here Fano pretended to disdain the Moho story, telling us that only Maupiti mothers trafficked with the god, and then only to scare disobedient children into eating their tarotops. But when we entered a nearby rocky cave and walked about 30 feet back into the darkness, we noticed our guide remained outside.

We visited several *maraes*, too, small editions of others we had seen, and equally shunned by the devout present-day populace. Maupiti had been an independent kingdom before annexation by the French, but its customs were identical with islands farther east which were dominated by the early Tahitian and Raiatean conquerors. Autonomy had been possible and practicable because Maupiti's location and relative size made it the least desirable of the high islands in the group.

One of Fano's insistent demands was that we stay on at least until conditions were ripe for a fish drive. Within two or three weeks wind and tide would be just right and the entire island would then turn out to show us their greatest cooperative event. But our anxiety to sail on was too strong. Each day now our Bora Bora water supply was getting lower in *Viator's* tanks. Maupiti, sadly enough, has no streams, and while we were there the fresh-water situation was practically nil. Springs which sometimes bubbled from the base of the cliffs were all dry because of a long period without rains. Two families sported tin roofs and had barrels of rain water; these were being carefully conserved against a possible prolongation of the dry spell. Meanwhile, all were depending on coconut water for both cooking and thirst quenching.

At last our cue came to be off. Especially early one morning we were aroused by the South Sea's most primitive sound—Fano was standing upon the nearby shore blowing a series of blasts upon a conch shell. He was calling all passengers to his father's ship. The wind had accommodatingly swung around to facilitate negotiation of the pass, and the old man had suddenly decided to sail.

The Ninth Island—Mopelia

BY NOON we too were on our way, and by nightfall had put Maupiti far below our eastern horizon. We were sailing right into the west now, with wind full astern and the square sail set and pulling furiously. At the present rate we hoped to cover the hundred miles to Mopelia sometime the following morning.

Watches were distributed so that Hazel's would best fit in with meal getting. She had the 8:00 a.m. to 12:00 watch, which put her at the tiller after breakfast and off in time to prepare lunch—then a chance to relax all afternoon before preparing the evening snack. Harry took the 12:00 to 4:00 and I the 4:00 to 8:00. Although he and I didn't have the cooking to think about, we always kept thoroughly busy between winks, shifting sail and policing the boat.

As a matter of fact, during part of that first afternoon's run I thought I might not have any cooking to worry about at all then, or for the remainder of the voyage. We had done so many gymnastics with the square sail, getting it on deck and getting it rigged, that I found myself face to face with that malady which sailors hesitate to confess even to their mothers. Those little equilibrium things in my ears had become confused and were transmitting their confusion to my stomach. And as I tried to swallow my pride and other things, there was Hazel, fresh as a daisy, seated at the tiller, calmly munching away at a platter of coconut fudge she had made during the early-morning hours.

When I had first talked to Harry about the advisability of having a sailorette aboard his craft, he had been prompt to say that sex had nothing to do with seamanship—a fragile girl might at times be better than a boatload of men. As I sat on the cabin trunk, wondering how soon the last trace of green would leave my face, I wondered very frankly what we were doing 8,000 miles from home in a Tom Thumb craft with an inch of planking between us and the sharks. I even tried to upbraid myself for getting my dear wife involved in the voyage, but from that train of thought I could get no satisfaction, for at the moment she was the only soul aboard thoroughly enjoying herself. I have always contended since that it was the fudge ordeal that did it to me, for after Hazel had eaten her last piece and thrown the crumbs overboard, I felt fine again.

All of us were looking forward to the second day at sea. After weeks of cruising among the high islands we were now on a hop that might require some decimal-point navigation. We had a secret feeling, of course, that we were headed directly for the atoll and, whether we used the sextants or not, would hit it right on the nose. But some current or other might be heading us off and if so, noon sights could be depended upon to correct our error. So the morrow was awaited with keen interest.

Then, to quote the silent pictures, "came the dawn." The wind was as strong and constant as before, but after only a brief moment of sunlight, high, racing storm clouds took over the heavens as completely as though a crazy-quilt had been drawn over us. All sight taking was suddenly out of the question. Nothing to do but hold our course and cross our fingers. If we made the islet before dark, all would be fine. If we didn't, we must spend the night listening for coral breakers.

By 4:00 p.m. the wind had swung around to the beam and we took off the square sail. By five it was so dark we couldn't have seen Mopelia a hundred yards away in any direction. We shortened sail further and then hove to, hoping that a clear morning ahead would present us with our quarry—or that a clear day would allow us to use the sextants and find it, in case it didn't turn up on schedule.

But the morning of the third day was every bit as mocking as its predecessor. Our log indicator showed that we had come 126 miles—26 miles too far! Somewhere, in some direction other than straight ahead, was that pinpoint on the chart, Mopelia. In a drizzle of rain we sat around the cockpit in consultation. Blind man's buff was a cinch compared to this. By process of elimination we endeavored to deduce our position. If we had swung too far to the north or south in the clutches of an uncharted current, we were apt to be anywhere on the compass.

We finally decided to play our hunches—and we had one hunch in common. We all shared the feeling we were too far north and west. If we kept going as we were, we would ultimately arrive at the Philippines—if our groceries lasted that long. To be sure, this ocean is dotted with islands, but no less a sailor than Magellan himself sailed across the entire South Pacific from Tierra del Fuego to the Philippines without sighting an inch of dry land.

In one way, our hunches probably were almost as good as any sights we might take. We had had no time check on the chronometers since leaving Papeete (seven weeks before), and we could have only an approximately calculated position at best. We had hoped to get a time tick from the Frenchman's radio on Bora Bora, but when we spoke to him about it he said he got his time once a week from the Papeete Concert Programme, a source Hazel aptly characterized as hit or miss both as to time and music.

We came about, fixing our compass on SSE, and mentally put Mopelia on trial. If it persisted in hiding away through another 24-hour period, we might check it off our itinerary and impatiently strike for Rarotonga, approximately 500 miles southwest. Then, too, there was the possibility the atoll had settled below the surface as the result of a recent submarine upheaval—an exciting idea conjured up no doubt from childhood memories of the *National Geographic!*

It was a long day, this third day out of Maupiti, and most of it continued wet. We did, however, have a couple of hours respite from the rain in the early afternoon, and Hazel, our little builder-upper, decided to read aloud from Count von Luckner's one-time best seller *The Sea Devil,* just in case we should never lay eyes upon our elusive atoll. The book, it will be remembered, was a journal of the adventures of a German raider which had been plundering in the Pacific during World War I.

It was on an early morning in the summer of 1917 that Luckner had brought his camouflaged gunboat off the pass of the very atoll we were looking for:

> Words fail me when I try to describe Mopelia's beauties. From the blue ocean rises a mass of green palms. The sunlight flows in the green. It somehow even seems to turn the sunlight green, and against the dark blue of the sky, the sunlight seems to be drawing the green island out of the water and the soft south wind carries the scent of flowers far out to sea. It is the greeting of the island and we inhale it deeply.
>
> Here was a typical coral atoll—the kind you dream about. A circular reef studded with waving palms and within the reef a lovely, placid lagoon. The coral shore was snow white and, with the sun's rays reflecting from it, it looked like a sparkling jewel set in an alabaster ring, like emeralds set in ivory. There were coral terraces below the water. The shallower ones were white or pale green, and as you peered deeper into the water you saw every conceivable tint of green and blue, sea green, emerald green, blue green, azure blue, sapphire blue, navy blue, violet.
>
> As we sailed nearer and nearer that alluring coral shore, we saw flowers among the palms, flowers of all colors, and immense numbers of orchids. The hues of the flowers were reflected in the water over the white coral that deepened and turned green....

It might be unfair, perhaps, to criticize the swashbuckling Count too severely for going poetic at this stage of his narrative. The *Seeadler* had covered a tremendous lot of ocean before writing her last chapter at Mopelia, and skipper and crew were weary and half sick as they approached the atoll. The raider had, since running the British blockade in December 1916, logged 30,000 miles, and Luckner and his companions selected Mopelia because some of the company were showing signs of beri-beri and scurvy. The remote islet would, they thought, be a safe hideaway in which to forage for greens and fresh water before continuing their marauding round the world to the west.

What they could not guess was the relative security of anchorage. The *Seeadler* was far too enormous to get through Mopelia's single pass into the shelter of the lagoon, so she of necessity had to be cable tethered from the leeward coral of the outer reef. It was this tethering that proved her undoing. Three days later a freak tidal wave tossed the fortified clipper ship clear over the outer reef and high up on the beach. The great masts snapped over the side like match sticks. Tons of water poured into the hatches to flood the maze of secret rooms below deck.

Days before, when Luckner was laying his course for Mopelia, he had made the remark that in this locality "wind and current were known to be as treacherous as anywhere in the world." Could he have conceived, in advance, of such things as tidal waves his *Seeadler* might have lived to pursue her nefarious career.

Luckner had much more to say about Mopelia, and Hazel's reading made us increasingly anxious about the whole thing. Certain passages made us increasingly confused, too, for it was hard to believe that such an infinitesimal spot on the chart could boast so many incomparable wonders.

Luckner, in his few days on the atoll prior to escaping by small boat to the Cook Islands, noted things which topped all South Sea phenomena within our experience. Especially on the subject of wild life was he illuminating. Besides giant hermit crabs which "swarmed the island like a carpet" and accounted for the death of a dachshund mascot, there were "hundreds" of turtles underfoot. Even queer birds, butterflies, and glowworms contributed to the Alice-in-Wonderland qualities of the island. Luckner's story of them is best told by himself:

> Flashing birds of paradise flew from palm to palm. Gorgeous humming birds with green and yellow breasts darted among the branches. With every flower there seemed to be a great butterfly. The whole island was aglow with butterflies. They floated on wide, beating wings of greens, violets and reds.
>
> Once, in the middle of the night, I was awakened by a small, sharp, repeated sound—knick, knick, knack. It was the opening of tropical flowers. I went outside and there I saw the lovely Queen of Night, which blossoms by the light of the tropical stars. It is a great, gorgeous bloom, eight or ten inches across. There were thousands of them. Scores of glowworms far brighter than any we know, hovered above each, eager to catch the magnificent perfume that the opening of Queen of Night gives forth. In the darkness I could see the flowers only by the light of the glowworms. On every side were these eerie nocturnal lights, a dancing lamp of gathered glowworms illuminating each flower.
>
> In that unearthly gleaming, like a kind of moonlight only stranger, the odorous petals shone with the ghostly nuances of their naturally flaming colors, white, crimson, sapphire blue, violet blue.

This was pretty strong fare for the crew of the *Viator*. Absorbing such stuff was apt to bring on beriberi. Or jim-jams. And we couldn't even find the darned atoll.

Then, at nightfall, we had a signal of encouragement. A score of frigate birds came wheeling low over our wake as if to urge us on. Although frigates are often known to reconnoiter hundreds of miles from their base, we chose to believe that these were easy-going fellows, killing time not far from homes and families.

As a sickly moon tried to thrust its way through the rainy sky, we took down the foresail, flattened the main, and backed the jib for another night at hove-to. The *Viator* rode hove-to just like a little duck upon the water. In the gentle breeze the boat would fall off a couple of points, sail along a few minutes, then come up into the wind to repeat the performance over again. At first we thought we would all sit up and listen for crashing surf, but by 10:00 o'clock Harry and I left the deck to Hazel and turned in to the gentle clatter of the blocks.

Six hours later, when Harry shook me at the end of his watch, I knew even before he spoke that our quest was fruitless as before. "Keep your ears open for that surf," he whispered, as I slid out of my bunk.

For some reason I felt a bit restless as I took over. Although it was still quite dark, the prospect of sitting still, attempting to keep awake and listen for trouble ahead, didn't appeal to me at all. I took a couple of turns around the deck, looking for things to do, then climbed out on the end of the bowsprit and fancied for an instant I could see a low hulk just ahead. It disappeared. I next hoisted the foresail and flattened it down so we wouldn't sail. Then, after a 20-minute struggle with the log line, which had become fouled around the rudder, I decided to have a single-handed cruise for myself. I loosened all the sheets and got under way, noting only casually that I was pointing due north.

Never will I forget the next couple of hours as long as I live. With my two companions dead to the world below, what could they know or care of the courses I chose? We were dozens of miles off our true course anyway, and it might be a week before we got a sun or star sight. I would forget our self-imposed navigating discipline and play hide-and-seek with the rain squalls through the remainder of my watch.

Before long I had picked up a squall that drove *Viator* along, rail under—a few miles farther north. Then, as increasing daylight brought more visibility, I changed course from time to time, trying to skirt the areas of heaviest rain and circumnavigate the blackest clouds. It was great sport working to outguess the elements, and with a whole ocean for playground I was so absorbed in the feeling of absolute freedom I felt like shouting for joy.

It must have been around 6:30 that I attempted my flashiest maneuver. Not more than five miles to the south, between two great masses of black cloud forms, some sunlight was slanting down upon the gray water. The effect was not unlike a famous photograph of sunbeams playing through the tall windows of Grand Central Station. If *Viator* could get through that opening, I mused, before the clouds above it clashed together, we would find our promised land. It was an omen— and a good one.

For some reason the thought of Grand Central linked up another New York thought in my mind. I suddenly beheld a vision of those window displays of perfect green vegetables featured by the Restaurants Longchamps. Giant raw string beans and peas the size of marbles danced before my eyes. We were off for the land of sunbeams and greens—racing to get through the bright portals before they were closed forever against us and our little boat.

Land could easily have been anywhere but, lo and behold, land lay just beyond the sun-bathed portals! All hands were piped on deck with the loudest "Land ho!" boomed in those waters since the days of Herman Melville.

A low string of faded green lay across our bow which, at a half hour's distance, might have been anything but a coconut isle. It suggested most, an area of Nevada desert covered with scrubby brush.

Only as we came close in did we note dark-pink coral against the sea and countless thousands of waving palms against the sky. We were able to peer through a sparsely planted area into a circular blue lagoon beyond, and to make out a tiny column of smoke on the far side approximately five miles away. We picked our way along a breaking surf until we came to some rusted tanks and twisted hulks of engine which flanked a small, swiftly flowing passageway.

Our greeting at Mopelia was something less than *Viator* had been accustomed to expect. For hours we sailed up and down before the pass, until like a prom queen suddenly forced to sit out a dance, we felt completely crushed. Far across the inner lagoon the wisp of smoke continued to curl upward above the coconut fronds but nothing happened.

Our *Pilot Book* told us about Mopelia's flat appearance and made mention of a "single dangerous pass, inaccessible even to the smallest vessels, without the greatest care." Nothing more. Although the *See-adler's* remains had lain on the reef for so many long years, no mention of her had found its way into the descriptive text.

We eventually got inside the lagoon, but not until late afternoon, when two young Polynesians in an outrigger shot through the pass and paddled alongside just as we were becoming reconciled to spending another night at sea.

Neither of the lads could have been more than twenty. Strong and handsome they were, too, and so excited about our arrival they climbed over every inch of *Viator*, admiring and repeating "maitai" again and again. They hadn't come from the far side, where the smoke curled, but had been gathering eggs on the lagoon edge of a bird islet which was part of the atoll's ring, three or four miles to the south. We had been invisible from the rookery where they worked, and only as they started paddling back to camp were we sighted.

With one lad at the tiller and the other on the bowsprit waving and barking Tahitian phrases over his shoulder, we crashed through the line of breakers between some rather menacing coral heads and threaded our way into a craterlike central basin to anchor off a group of thatched houses not far from our point of entry. Still, surprisingly enough, we noted no signs of life anywhere about us and wondered more than ever about the smoke across the water.

To make matters more mysterious, our young greeters indicated nothing about going ashore but with voluble signs explained that many people would come from the direction of the smoke and we must wait. So wait we did, passing out cigarettes and playing our phonograph until a white speck started toward us from the opposite shore.

Through our glasses the white speck eventually grew into an eight-oared whale boat loaded with natives, but not until it was very close were we certain of the kind of reception we were to receive. Before the boat came within earshot its occupants looked belligerent enough to cook and eat us. As we watched them draw closer we realized they had been pulling their hearts out, and the ugly looks which flashed over their shoulders as they rowed, were merely facial contortions due to extra effort. When they pulled alongside and leaped aboard, two score strong (just about sinking us with their weight), every sweating face was wreathed in smiles.

"I am Roo Fiu, manager of Mopelia for the *Syndicat Français,* and I welcome you in the name of Mr. Miller of Papeete and Paris," said a huge, black-spectacled fellow who had been helmsman for the boarders. "This is Timi and Ropati and Tioti and Etera and Rangora and . . ."

"Wait a minute," said Harry, linking up a familiar sound with a vaguely familiar face. "What do you say this fellow's name is?"

"Etera."

"Hello Etera—does our boat look familiar?"

"Sure, same size as *Svaap.* I sail yatch *Svaap* around world long time ago with Mr. Robinson. Pilot plenty other yatch Tahiti-Bora Bora, Tahiti-Raiatea, Tahiti-Moorea. 'Scuse me, I fix hankors."

And the mate of *Ten Thousand Leagues Over the Sea* was in the water in a flash, refastening our hooks to the coral according to his own ideas. Pot-bellied and gray-thatched, the fifty-year-old brown billikin was as agile as any youngster. He stayed under an incredibly long time before reappearing to announce, "Hankors okay now." While he was thus occupied, we gleaned some quick highlights on Mopelia from Roo.

There were *in toto* 51 souls in the community, all engaged, as the spirit moved them, in some phase of the drying and shipping of coconut meat. Thirty-eight young Tahitians did most of the heavy chores. Nine wives tended to housekeeping and fought occasionally over the single men, three children contributed in the lighter work, and Etera was the official cook.

The reason the village inside the pass appeared deserted was because all had adjourned to the far side some days previously to make copra. We weren't visible from the work camp until we came to anchor off the village, and had it not been for the egg gatherers we might have sailed up and down outside considerably longer without attracting notice.

Roo had fought in France in the first World War and was one of the few Papeete volunteers who came back alive. Now, on Mopelia, he loved the peace and solitude that it spelled for his declining years. He had been on the atoll seven years without respite, and didn't expect to go to Tahiti on vacation for three more. He had a two-year contract with the Tahiti Syndicate, and his renewals had been regularly and enthusiastically taken up. Twice annually a small trading schooner sailed to the island and anchored where we lay. It brought canned beef, butter, sugar, and the all-important tobacco from Papeete, and took away between 50 and 60 tons of copra each trip.

Only one other yacht had paid Mopelia a call in Roo's memory, and he couldn't for the life of him remember her name. She had arrived some six years before, carried three men, and was about 10 feet longer than *Viator*. He had gone outside and piloted her in, and he vividly recalled that the largest shark he had ever seen accompanied the boat to the pass. We learned later that Roo was not given to exaggeration, but at the time his description seemed too fantastic to be believed. The monster glided alongside the yacht, he said, with snout opposite the bowsprit and tail even with the helmsman. It must have been something over 32 feet in length, because all agreed the creature was longer than our over-all measurement. Roo said it had been sighted near the pass on a couple of recent occasions and was no legend.

Then, abruptly changing the subject, Roo went on with the speech of welcome.

"It is a tradition on Mopehaa," he said, using the old native name for the atoll, "that if ever a yacht comes here, we do everything within our power to make our guests happy. I invite the lady and her husband to use my humble house, and we have another house where we promise to make the captain comfortable."

So we moved bags and baggage ashore, and a charming month commenced, different from anything we had so far experienced.

James Hall had been most emphatic in his description of life on an isolated atoll. The very remoteness, together with the day-by-day sameness, adds up to make for a charm that relaxes one beyond anything in his experience, he said.

We were particularly entranced by those night skies in which all the stars were sharply visible. On such nights we felt we were seeing a privileged new part of the heavens. Yet here were all the familiar navigation stars of the southern hemisphere, their piercing rays pinpointing constellations known through antiquity: Acrux, at the peak of the Cross; Betelgeux and Bellatrix and Rigel of the Belt of Orion; Aldebaran, Capella, Alphard, Regulus, and Dubhe; Pollux, Procyon, and Sirius—and Scorpio, the great hook which the fishing god Maui tossed into the heavens after he had finished dragging up islands from the depths of the Pacific. Yes, we agreed with Hall that there are parts of the world which seem "planned for the spiritual refreshment of mankind—places from which one carries away a new serenity and a sense of yearning for beauty, satisfied."

We hated to take over Roo's house so completely. But he would hear of no other arrangement, so Hazel and I found ourselves in as tidy a little thatched apartment as there was in the South Seas. Red-and-blue-flowered *pareu* cloth covered a table and hung in the doorway, and a floor of snow-white coral pebbles glistened in the reflected light from the lagoon. The entire little settlement was neat as a pin. The smooth sand between the dwellings was kept as clean as a billiard table. Little paths led here, there, and everywhere, and they were all edged with pieces of bleached coral. All the nearby coconut trees were artistically circled at the base with coral slabs, and on every hand evidences of civic pride reflected Roo's taste for beauty and order.

Of course, one could look in vain for Herr Luckner's birds of paradise, butterflies, etc., etc., etc. Roo was much amused when we showed him the passages in the book we had read.

"Mopelia has never known a flower or any of those other fancy things," he boomed, white teeth flashing. "But let me show you something by your front door which you may have missed." He then showed us a frail little green stem that grew from a mound of dirt just beside our threshold.

"There is the only *tiare* bush ever to grow on Mopehaa. It, and the soil it grows in, came on the last schooner from Tahiti many months ago. If it blooms while you are here, I intend to present the first blossom to Madame," turning to Hazel with a bow, "including my compliments."

Never did time seem to fly as during our weeks on Mopelia. As the days passed we came more and more to feel at home, and we entered into a routine of activities as though we had been residents of the atoll all our lives. Life on the islet revolved around Etera's ringing of the gong—a large *Seeadler* shell casing which dangled by a wire from a tree. There was not a clock anywhere—he sounded off entirely by intuition. Around 6:30 each morning the bell rang to summon everyone to breakfast. It rang again for noon and evening meals.

Etera was nothing short of an Oscar of the Waldorf around his outdoor kitchen. He maintained two large ground ovens in which several varieties of fish, wrapped in plaited palm leaves, baked continuously amidst piles of red-hot coral rock. He also had contrived a corrugated-iron oven in which he baked fresh bread daily and on occasion turned out a batch of pies filled with canned fruits from our larder on *Viator*. His fuel was never a problem for the inexhaustible coconut husk was ever at arm's reach.

And what, one may well ask, does one do for greens amidst these continuing menus of sea foods, raw, baked, or souffléed? For greens, one must be content with a dish which only the richest of Indian potentates could afford to serve at every meal. For greens we ate our fill each day of a little item once listed in Maxim's of Paris as "heart of palm salad— $75.00 per portion." Heart of palm is the upper central shoot of a young coconut tree. The shoot is about four feet long and three or four inches thick, and is so truly the "heart" of the palm that its removal kills the tree. The natives are careful to mark out for salads only those trees which promise to be nonbearing of nuts and thus worthless to a copra atoll. We thought the dish tasted like a very tender and sweet celery.

On one day that was a particularly red-letter one for us, we joined an expedition which was canoeing out to the farthest bird islet for fresh eggs. The mission took an entire day, because we were so engrossed with what we saw that after we had filled one of the canoes with about a thousand of the pinkish-speckled eggs, we stayed on.

The birds were a variety of sooty tern, and the eggs, about two-thirds the size of hen's eggs, lay everywhere about on the sand. By gathering eggs only from an area that had been cleared on a previous visit, we could be sure that those we took were fresh. Another test was to toss the eggs into the lagoon shallows and discard the "floaters" as inedible.

On the way home we beached the canoes on a frigate-bird motu and had a look at one of the busiest of south-sea rookeries. The sky was black with the giant birds taking off and landing—screaming and beating the air with their powerful wings. Frigate eggs (highly inedible, by the way) are laid in branches of a sort of sage-brush variety of tree. The nests of twigs repose about five feet above the sand and contain one egg each. In some nests a baby frigate sits in place of the egg. Babies are as large as chickens yet are still unable to fly. When approached, they unfailingly up-chuck lunches of pink squid. The bushes were full of adult male frigates left to guard the young while the mothers flew to sea for the squid which they hijack from other birds. Some of the males were so slow to rise from the nests that we caught them by the wings and let them go again in a din of squawking.

Near the frigate rookery we encountered a young octopus in a rock-bound pool. He was about four feet between tentacle tips. We studied him for an hour and marveled at his constant change of shape and mastery of protective coloration. He was so frightened, he tried all manner of ruses to get away. He could flatten out and become the exact color and texture of the sand, or turn purple and pink and sprout barbs to become part and parcel of the coral. Sometimes he streamlined himself and rocketed across the pool with incredible speed—again, he would execute a sort of eight-footed gallop and charge the water with murky coloring. When one of the natives suggested spearing him for supper we suggested that the creature, having been frightened nearly to death, had earned its freedom.

Not far from the octopus pool, Harry made a discovery that was another highlight of the day's wanderings. Gently rolling to and fro in a lagoon basin was a corked bottle with a message inside. The scrawly note which we extracted read:

> H.M.S. Dunedin, 100 miles from Nuka Hiva. If found state where and when and mail to E. C. Elliot, Dunedin, New Zealand.

The bottle was 600 miles from its starting point, which is a fair indication that currents are strong in the South Pacific.

We thought Mr. Elliot's note was a bit abrupt—no "please" or "thank you" on it. And it assumed that there was a mailbox on every coconut tree. Hazel thought that perhaps a copy of Emily Post was the thing to mail to Mr. Elliot. But the message was faithfully dispatched some months later by mail steamer from the Cook Islands, and we hoped it would bring joy to Dunedin.

About halfway home the boys again beached the canoes. They walked us across some fringing reef to a section of outer beach piled high with the pieces of an ill-fated treasure ship. Many years ago, in the island's sketchy past, a three-masted schooner, the *Retriever*, was deliberately run upon the reef and wrecked here. Her cargo, the story goes, consisted of two and one-half million dollars in gold and silver bullion, plundered from a South American church vault and brought thither for safe burial.

Odd bits of teak planking, railing, and companionway much rounded by the elements were strewn over a half-mile radius, high and dry among the palms. As for the treasure, we could only see that a number of people had taken stock in its existence. So many great pits were dug by the curious, down through the years, that portions of the atoll looked like the outskirts of a Colorado mining town.

Back at the "village," the eggs safely delivered to Etera, we turned our attention to Roo's turtle-conservation program. In the lagoon shallows more than a hundred baby turtles are kept in floating cages as part of a turtle-propagation idea begun by Roo several years before. The plan is roughly this: for every turtle a native raises to maturity and sets free, he is allowed to send another away to the Papeete market to be sold and credited to his account. As all natives participate in the scheme, all share equally in the sales.

At turtle time (only in November, Herr Luckner notwithstanding) men hide along the outer beach night after night and wait for mother turtles to clamber in over the reef. Sometimes they wait two weeks without seeing one, sometimes they spot a dozen in their first week's vigil. Always their job is to lie completely hidden until eggs have been laid, for the eggs are the important thing, and killing the female turtle is rarely attempted.

Turtle eggs are about the size of ping-pong balls, and 150 are often laid at one sitting. Staking the claims, even after having witnessed the egg-laying procedure, is difficult, because a mother turtle is a great pantomimist and will go to no end of trouble to disguise the caching of her embryonic young. Often she will waddle several hundred yards along the high beach, digging a series of dummy holes and going through the motions of laying, just to throw interlopers off the track. These fake mounds not only fool the men but, around hatching time three months later, hundreds of hermit crabs encircle them in wait for the tender, spiderlike turtles they hope to intercept on the dash to the sea.

This dash of the newly hatched turtles to the sea must be the most pathetically one-sided struggle in the world. (If they could only be taught to dash to the inner lagoon instead!) Should any manage to outflank the gauntlet of big red hermit crabs, the odds are 100 to one they will be snapped up by sea birds before they have traveled 10 feet; should a lucky one reach the water, the chances are one in 100 he will swim safely past the waiting sharks. All South Sea killers can sense turtle time, and today man is apparently the turtle's only true friend. Thanks to man, 100 lagoon-raised Mopelia turtles are set free each year —turtles formidable enough, by virtue of their 10-inch backs, to hold their own.

Fisherman-in-chief of Mopelia was Atau, a stocky old fellow who was able to produce on short notice any fish delicacy demanded. He could gather a sack of lobster, moi, or cavelli in just about the time it takes an American housewife to roll a wire basket through an A. & P.

Helping Atau with his fishing chores each day was one way in which we tried to prove ourselves useful in the community. To him, of course, the procedure was routine—to us it was an experience far removed from any "duty" we had ever before performed.

Early one morning, after an especially piquant breakfast of bird's-egg soufflé, garnished with grated coconut, coffee, and canned jam from the *Viator*, Atau armed the three of us with spears as well as the usual short hooks and lines. Then he led us around the mainland to a section of the outer lagoon where scarcely a foot of water covered about an acre of flat sandy bottom. This we came to know as Shark Pond, and it offered thrills aplenty. Here, medium-sized sharks came to sun-bathe in the tepid shallows. It was claimed that since nothing over five feet in length could swim with ease at this depth, we were safe from man-eaters.

Atau's heavy iron-barbed spear flew with deadly accuracy. Any black triangle of fin within 25 or 30 feet of his throwing arm was as good as a trophy of the hunt before he even wound up to throw. The sharks were quite lethargic in their movements until they became aware of what was going on—then they really tore up the water around us. They rarely came very close, but to us, at any distance, they seemed horrific. After Atau had thrown about a dozen upon the beach, he set about slitting their bellies. From each sleek white paunch slid a bucketful of tiny, bright-colored lagoon fish. To emphasize his antipathy for the wolves of the sea he tossed them back for eager brethren to devour.

When is a shark really dead? We thrust a spear handle into the mouth of one whose belly had been slit, and the jaw closed with a bang. Three double rows of teeth clamped themselves into the wood, to snap off like brittle glass and remain embedded as the hardwood pole was wrenched free.

Nothing to do but work and play. And on Mopelia the workers were never too tired to play. Every evening, to the accompaniment of a dozen pairs of hands beating the hard-packed sand at the lagoon's edge, dancers outlined against the starlit sky wove rhythmic patterns upon the beach. Sometimes the steady thump thump thump—thump thump thump of hands smiting the earth was augmented by light tapping on blocks carved from coconut trunks. On other occasions the muffled sound of a heavy drumstick made of braided husk fibre could be heard beating a tattoo on a section of galley oven salvaged from the *Seeadler*. This soft boom, mingled with the far-away thud of the surf on the outer reef, cast a spell of primitive enchantment around the silhouetted dancing figures, making us forget that they were the everyday personalities we had grown to know so well.

Each afternoon a fleet of miniature sailing canoes was launched in the near lagoon and, like so many happy children, the entire citizenry of the isle scampered around, watching and participating in the races. The little ships were beautifully carved, and with their brightly colored *pareu* sails they made a flamboyant splash of color as they darted about, heeling against the steady trade wind.

Then one day we had one of the most surprising experiences that could possibly happen to Americans far from home. We knew the night before that something was astir, because Roo had come aboard *Viator* as we were making our nightly check-up and winding the chronometers, and asked if he could borrow the ship's flags. He also wanted a revolver and a Very pistol.

"Captain, I am sorry to bother you for these things—and I am sorry I cannot tell you why I need them. There will be a committee come to wake you all at dawn tomorrow and then you will see."

We couldn't imagine what our friend was planning. The three of us watched him paddle ashore with the things he had requested, and for a long time we sat talking and gazing at the twinkling stars before we climbed into *Okay* and started for the beach. All was so quiet as we pulled the boat up at the lagoon's edge we might have been alone.

As our paths parted we exchanged a few whispers and decided to give up trying to guess what it was all about, get a good night's sleep, and trust to our first impression that Roo had an honest face.

People troubled with insomnia should try an atoll. In spite of our uncertain conjecturing as to what the morrow would hold, we slept soundly.

It seemed but an instant until we were awakened by the clanging of Etera's gong. We dressed quickly and emerged to find a smiling "committee" of three, clad completely in store clothes and nervously twisting blue trading-schooner berets in their hands. Motioning us to follow, they put on their hats and marched over to Harry's door; he joined the procession and we filed down to the beach.

The beach was a sight to behold. During the night two coconut-trunk flagstaffs had been raised, and at the peak of one flew the Tricolor of France—on the other the Stars and Stripes whipped triumphantly in the wind. Roo, clad in white shirt and shorts, stood at rigid attention between the flagpoles as we approached. Drawn up in a semicircle around him, dressed in Sunday best, was the entire populace of Mopelia. A sort of dais had been arranged back of Roo, and to it we were ushered, still completely baffled as to what was going on.

Then, looking straight ahead over the ranks of his audience and never once shifting his eyes in our direction, Roo suddenly pointed *Viator's* revolver skyward and loosed a salvo of 45-caliber ammunition into the blue heavens above.

As the echo of the last shot died away, 51 throats commenced to sing:

As the song went on through the final stanza and we watched the straining faces striving on the highest notes, it was all that we could do to hold back the tears of emotion that welled in our eyes. Unbeknown to us, Roo had been secretly drilling these people for weeks on the music of *The Star Spangled Banner*. He had remembered the tune from his war days in France, and although he never knew the words, he proceeded to invent Tahitian lyrics that the islanders could understand. He had drilled them so thoroughly that every voice was confident. Each and every soul combined to make our anthem ring in the palm fronds of that distant outpost of Empire, until the very air was vibrant with Francis Scott Key's eloquent tribute to Old Glory.

It was Bastille Day, July 14.

There was one amusing twist to the ceremony. Hazel, sensing the formality of the occasion, had put aside her slacks and worn a dress for the one and only time on the voyage. Meanwhile, the women of Mopelia had been busily cutting up their *pareu* cloths to make slacks such as they had seen on Hazel. So, when Hazel appeared in a dress and surprised everyone, she was confronted in turn by a bevy of ladies in slacks who surprised her.

Of all places, Mopelia is the spot we have marked for a return visit. Roo may be gone when we again slide through the little pass but someone of like caliber will administer the affairs of the group of childlike people who tend the palms and devote most of their time to dance and song. The people on such a place just cannot change. Every beautiful quality of the Polynesian reaches full flower in such a setting.

We never missed the things promised in the Luckner saga — we found an abundance of beauty in the souls of the natives.

The Last Island—RAROTONGA

BY July 18, pleasant as it all was on Mopelia, the time had come to shove off for the 500-mile passage to Rarotonga. Roo and his friends plied the longboat to and from our anchorage, restoring the various belongings we had gradually piled up ashore and were now carefully stowing once again for deep water. While Hazel and Harry took a series of sights to try to check the chronometers, the rest of us busied ourselves lashing everything movable on deck and taking a final look over the rigging. It was a truly touching farewell; we shook hands all around, received a final huge gift of drinking nuts, and presented Roo and his boys with our phonograph and a pile of their favorite records. Willing hands dived into the coral to retrieve our anchor and place it on deck, and at the final moment Ropati and the small boy Ataati came aboard to pilot us to the pass, their outrigger in tow.

After recent days and nights of a wind which blew the top off the lagoon, the day we chose to sail seemed perfect. Tiny white-caps dappled the lagoon, the sun was shining brightly from a very clear blue sky, and the threatening weather of the *maraamu* seemed to have passed for another month.

The starter refused to work and we spun the motor into purring activity by hand. Ropati, Hazel, and I manned the cockpit while Harry conned from the bowsprit and little Ataati crouched high up the foremast waving his brown arms to port and starboard as the purple coral patches loomed here, there, and seemingly everywhere in our path. As Ropati threw the helm this way and that, snaking the boat toward the pass, the 3:00 p.m. sun glared full in our eyes—only Ataati, aloft, could see where we were going.

At last we were in the pass. Our two pilots made a quick scramble into their canoe and paddled furiously toward a back eddy and the safety of the lagoon. The giant roll of the incoming swell parted squarely on our bows—the fast current and the full-throttled motor pushed the *Viator* through it like a thing bewitched. With three violent pitches that catapulted several coconuts from the cockpit down into the companionway, we were suddenly over deep water—the "permanent blue-black scrip" of the unearthly deep outside the barrier reef.

I put on the mainsail, Harry raised the jib and the foresail, and Hazel swung the ship onto south by west. Harry went below to cut the motor and shut off gas and seacocks, and in so doing missed a parting farewell from the depths as a grayish mass moved from under us and described a slow circle to windward. For an instant the sun shone just right for us to make out what it was—a tiger shark about 25 feet long.

The late afternoon breeze was very light—only enough to push us along about three knots. Soon Hazel was in the galley putting together a beef stew, and Harry and I in our off-pitch voices were roaring at the top of our lungs "The Road to Mandalay." (After an hour's yodeling we finally managed to get all the words and verses in their approximate sequence.)

The first night was more than idyllic. We weren't getting anywhere, navigationwise, but the conditions added up to more than anything we had ever read on sailing in the South Seas. Harry went off watch at 8:00 and went below to check over the chart a few minutes before turning in. Hazel was on from 8:00 to 12:00 while I slept. When I came on for the midnight-to-4:00 watch, the scene was such that we both sat silent for several minutes in awed wonder.

A moon with razor-sharp edges lighted the whole sea in such a manner that a million liquid mirrors seemed to be in motion around us. Between the myriad mirrors, black water — a black shining black, blacker than black—picked up a trillion dancing stars. The motion of the ship on the sea was gentle as only a child in a cradle can know. The soft breeze was by now just enough to keep steerage way, but the incandescent sails stayed as full as though they had been molded of plastic.

Globules of phosphorous tumbled from the bows, only to carom, bounce, dive, and divide into an infinity of seed pearls as the lee wash joined the wake under the counter astern.

All this was the first night out of Mopelia.

The second night was pretty much like it. But as someone has truly said, sailing conditions are never twice the same. By now a few clouds had appeared to clutter up the western sky. The motion of the boat was slightly different as the wind moved up a knot. The undulating mirrors and the star reflections had diminished perceptibly—and the barometer had taken a little drop. It was still so comfortable on deck that the three of us sat and gammed during part of Hazel's 8:00-to-12:00 watch. Light sweaters seemed enough to ward off the slight nip in the breeze, and the Southern Cross hung in its appointed place and made steering easy with all lights doused.

We talked of the size of the Pacific, its 64,000,000 square miles making it by far the vastest and loneliest of oceans. On the basis of depths alone the Pacific staggers the imagination. So many great pits have been plumbed in the Pacific, pits five and six miles deep, that it is not hard to believe the physicists who tell us that this greatest scar on the earth's surface once held the substance that is now the moon.

And here we were under the moon, the same moon that two billion years before is supposed to have filled the enormous crater in which the Pacific now supported our tiny craft.

We talked on into the night—as no doubt sailing folk under similar conditions have talked down through the centuries. Sometimes one thinks of a desert as a trackless waste, but of all the traveled expanses of this earth only the sea is really trackless. Here we were, crossing and recrossing furrows once cut by the early navigators, waters cleaved through all points of the compass by ancient war canoes; yet, as they left nothing to mark their passage, neither would we. Everywhere else that man has passed on the earth's earthy surface some mark has lingered on to say man was once there . . . a broken twig or a great city. Even in the polar north and south, small man-made cairns stand proud in frozen permanence. The sea alone refuses to record the path of man.

On the morning of the third day a check of the patent log showed but 86 miles. At 43 miles per day we would fetch Rarotonga about ten days hence! Harry managed to get two noon sights, then we straddled the bowsprit for half an hour trying to get snapshots of about 200 dolphins that were cavorting all around us. The flying fish, too, were busy in every direction, and great patterns of them crossed our wake in fighter formations, dazzling in their perfection of timing.

About midafternoon we first felt we were in for a change—the wind suddenly moved up to a full-sail breeze as the barometer took another jog downward. A parade of long, gray wind clouds with black, serrated edges passed in review across the eastern horizon. By dusk we were sure that we were in for a different kind of sailing than we had grown accustomed to expect. By the time Harry went off at 8:00 and Hazel took the helm, the rail was well under and the boat was once again needing constant and alert attention.

By the time I took over, Hazel was hanging on with all the strength she had—she found it was all she could do to hold the course, and by now spray was flying over the cockpit with every lunge. Just as Hazel stood up to leave the helm, a large wave collided with the beam, making an extra-loud rug-beater smack as it cascaded enough heavy spray aboard to make sure everything already soaked would surely stay soaked. Now a whipping rain was stinging our faces.

On this night there was no talk of the romance of the sea.

I had come up wearing oilskins over a lot of dry stuff underneath which included two sweaters. In half an hour I was drenched to the skin from head to foot and I knew, as one should always know, that when spray and rain are given a chance to operate with a real force of wind behind them, all oilskins are useless.

It was by now really cold—so cold that I took the bundle of wet blankets from the cockpit floor and wrapped myself up like an Indian. For a time I tried to steer lying down, with a loop of sheet from the high side around the tiller and my back against the cockpit coaming on the low side. But I didn't hold this position long, for as the lee rail buried itself progressively deeper, soon barrelfuls of heavy water were curling over the coaming and roaring along my prone form.

Fewer openings in the clouds overhead allowed the moonlight to filter through to light its old path abaft the port beam. And fewer openings in the black clouds over the bow revealed the Southern Cross to steer upon. Soon the Cross was completely obliterated by racing cloud forms and the wind was now a banshee's screech in the rigging.

I found that by sitting on the high side, with feet braced across the cockpit, and hunching over so the tiller lay tight against my chest, lock-pressed there by my arm pits, I could gaze down on the flickering binnacle and actually figure some sort of planned rhythm in the boat's movements. She seemed more in the groove now as fewer surprise crashes of solid water came over her. She was driving so hard that pitch and roll perceptibly diminished. Holding her on course, she heeled more and more until the peak strength of the wind drove her cabin coaming under, and green water intermittently covered the entire Marquesan canoe and threatened to strip the canvas cover off it. It grew increasingly colder and the seas were a black confusion of shapes on all sides. The resounding smacks on the exposed windward beam were noticeably heavier, and though they could not be heard, a jarring thud could be felt as the planking transmitted heavy shocks to the cockpit.

By the time Harry came on deck at 4:00 a.m. he was welcome to it. Just before he took over he put a flashlight on the log and yelled in my ear, "Thirty-eight miles! Averaging darn near eight knots!"

Harry's watch was a rough one. He said later that it seemed as though we were running through a series of gigantic tide rips. Certainly as he sailed her on into the dawn we folk below felt for all the world like two clappers in a cowbell. Such sliding, shifting, bouncing, gliding, careening, bumping, banging, and dizzy spinning is hard to imagine. Only by going over Niagara Falls in a barrel could one possibly duplicate the sensation one feels inside a small boat under the set of conditions we had the night before we sighted Rarotonga.

Harry sighted Rarotonga at dawn. It was the fifth day out of Mopelia. *Viator* had closed with the island by 8:30 a.m.—Hazel at the helm and Harry and I puttering with the stowage below. Next thing we heard from up topsides was a mighty cheer. We popped our heads out and discovered that Hazel had rounded *Viator* to off the pass and we were under the guns of a British man-of-war, the H.M.S. *Wellington*.

Later we were told that dozens of pairs of glasses had been trained on *Viator* for an hour before Hazel rounded to, and such expressions as "Lor, a blinkin' skimmin' dish with only a woman aboard" and "Bless me, a bloomin' single-'ander with a female Slocum in command" were passed along the rail. The *Wellington* was anchored to the coral ledge and tailing off to leeward over the deep water outside the reef. This is the only anchorage possible for anything big. The *Admiralty Pilot Directions* speak of Avarua Harbor thus: "The harbor has an evil reputation ... no vessel of more than 100 tons can enter."

In spite of Harry's best efforts at the motor not even a feeble cough or sputter came forth. A confusing surf was beating on the reef where we supposed the 50-foot pass to be, so we boxed back and forth near the warship several times until a pilot boat came out to us. In the launch were two grinning natives and the harbor pilot, O'Brien, who hopped aboard us with a hearty greeting:

"Wanting to come in, were you? We'll have you to the dockside in a jiffy."

As the launch towed us to the opening in the reef which we had not at first seen, O'Brien helped furl the stiff, salt-encrusted sails and shouted instructions to Hazel at the helm. Winding in the tortuous channel, not more than 15 feet wide in spots, O'Brien suddenly stopped his flow of commands to remark: "Sure, an' it seems awful funny talkin' this pilot lingo to a lady."

O'Brien pursed his lips in a low whistle when he examined our log and noted that we had done 170 miles in the past 24 hours. Then he proceeded to tell us that the island had felt the strength of a strong, unseasonal wind the night before. The edge of a baby hurricane had passed that way and had blown a tin roof off part of the Avarua customs shed and sent a number of small banana palms flying through the air.

While the customs official and doctor put the routine questions to us and took the mail bag which had been handed to us in Tahiti, marked "Rarotonga, direct," we feasted our eyes on a hundred crates of red-ripe tomatoes that sat on the dock waiting to be lightered out to the *Wellington*.

As we broke out a very wet and bedraggled yacht ensign over the stern, a messenger appeared from the Governor's residence inviting us to a ball that evening in honor of the officers of the *Wellington*. Feeling about twice as bedraggled as our flag, we regretfully declined and went instead to a little boarding house, where we washed the encrusted salt from our bodies and sank into the first beds with white linen sheets we had seen in months.

Speaking of salt, so much spray and heavy water had dashed aboard *Viator* on her slant southward that, once the decks were dry, we swept up a mound of salt crystals which was large enough to fill a small saucepan.

The contrast afforded by going from the French islands of the Tahiti group to the British colonial atmosphere of Rarotonga is as striking as one would expect if transported suddenly from a square dance in Reno to an afternoon tea at Claridge's in London.

All was colonial superefficiency and decorum on Rarotonga. The two hundred whites included the official families, the storekeepers, and always three or four wealthy sheep-raising families from New Zealand, who sojourn in Rarotonga the way United States tycoons take to Maine a few months each year. We saw much tennis, bowling on the green, and cricket. The 5,000 natives on the island all seemed to wear store clothes. We weren't to see a *pareu* on this Bond Street of the South Seas.

Rarotonga did, however, have its share of archaeological remains. We spent an afternoon wandering with natives through the Ngatangiia district. Here we saw the stone seats of the council chamber of the ancient nobles, and a crowning stone of the type we had seen in Raiatea.

On this tour we again felt the intense hospitality of the Polynesian toward any visitor who approaches his bamboo threshold. Occupants of one thatched house after another hailed us to sit upon their porch mats and drink of the ever-cool drinking nuts. Being an English-speaking island, conversation was easy everywhere, and as we stopped we picked up fragments of information which, pieced together, gave us something of the personality of the place.

On one porch our brown host gave us a long dissertation on the merits of the various rugby teams of Australia and New Zealand. The white administrators had long ago introduced rugby to the natives and built up some pretty hot competition between districts on the island. Also a number of powerful radio receivers in the town were regularly tuned in for running commentaries on championship games in Sydney and Wellington. One of the oddest things about following any of these events is the fact that the International Date Line lies but a few miles west of Rarotonga, and Saturday in the Cook Islands is Sunday in Australia. We shared with the natives the extreme sense of bafflement one experiences in listening to a radio on a Friday afternoon as it pours out play-by-play results of Saturday's game. Of course, it makes betting on tomorrow's games a cinch, and Harry and I almost made a couple of dollars from Hazel before she realized what we were up to.

Another soft-spoken host told us of his uncle and the missionary competition on Palmerston Island, in the northern Cooks:

"Few years ago Palmerston have 300 people belong London Missionary Society. My hunkle one. Everybody one. Then comes Seven Days (Seventh Day Adventist) boat—drops hankor. Seven Days missionary come ashore. My hunkle and all people pay before six shilling a year London Missionary Society. Seven Days man say three shilling plenty. My hunkle—everybody leave London Missionary *himine* house, join Seven Days church. Then God teach them big lesson. Hurricane come and make everybody poor."

As Huahine stood out in our minds for its stilt houses, Raiatea for its sailing canoes, and Bora Bora for its barter, Rarotonga was unforgettable as the rendezvous for the famed trading schooners of the Society Islands-Cook Island area. We had ridden the old *Denise* to Tubai but had been all too busy enjoying the ride to get to know the boat or her captain. In Rarotonga, with weeks to burn, we came to know the captains of the *Tiare Taporo* and the *Tagua* as intimately as one gets to know the skippers at a yacht-club anchorage at home.

Andy Thompson, captain of the *Tagua,* had called Rarotonga home for a good part of his fifty years. His native wife and five handsome children would go for weeks at a time without seeing or hearing from him as he made the 2,000-mile circuit to Penrhyn, Tahiti, and back. On this run, his main mission was carrying copra and livestock from, and trade goods to, the two dozen islands in the area.

The *Tagua* had been built in 1909 in Oakland, California, and sold to German traders in the Marshall Islands. She was seized near Guam in 1917 and put under New Zealand registry. The 110-ton schooner had been based at Rarotonga and skippered by Thompson since 1930.

Captain Thompson had left his birthplace, Brooklyn, to run away to the South Seas at such an early age he was hard put to it to remember any details of his boyhood. Only his accent remained to reveal his origin. Entirely self-taught, he had, by years of reading, an astounding all-around knowledge of things. He had collected what might be termed a "high-brow" library in the cramped captain's quarters of the ship. Aristophanes' comedies, all of Shakespeare, Plutarch's Lives were typical titles. He followed the contemporary scene from several years of *Readers Digests* packed in a sea chest at the end of his bunk.

He had seen quite a lot of the late Robert Dean Frisbie on Puka Puka and elsewhere. He once attempted to deliver a case of beer and two bottles of rum to author Frisbie, who refused to accept it. Frisbie waved the longboat away from shore, saying, "take it back, Andy — don't you know there is no more drinking on Puka Puka?" Then Frisbie proceeded to paddle out to the *Tagua* and spend 48 hours drinking the consignment before returning to shore. At that time Frisbie and his wife and nine kids were the sole population of Puka Puka.

Thompson also reminisced about a historic gam session with Nordhoff and Hall at Bohler's Bar in Tahiti. On this occasion they had talked eleven and a half hours about how civilization had gone to hell. Hall expounded upon how much he disliked machinery and how much pleasanter things must have been a hundred years before the machine age. When Thompson asked at what state of man's progress Hall would feel happiest, Hall responded, "I'd just keep improving things till we got to the Adam and Eve state."

Prominent on the wall of the *Tagua's* trading room was one of Thompson's proudest possessions, an oil painting by Captain Viggo Rasmussen, retired skipper of the famed *Tiare Taporo*. The brightly colored scene was a seascape, with Manihiki (Viggo's present home) in the background and the schooners *Tagua* and *Tiara Taporo* splitting tacks in the foreground.

The *Tiare Taporo* turned up off the pass late one afternoon, and after she had disgorged her passengers and livestock it was already dark. I had intended to go aboard and greet the captain but instead stood by the gangway in the deepening twilight just studying the old hull that had been eulogized by every South Pacific romantic from Beatrice Grimshaw to Frederick O'Brien. Queen of the South Seas trading schooners, she had, according to a score of books, been in every kind of adventure known to those seas, from pearl hijacking to hurricane fighting.

Suddenly a solitary figure came out of the shadows of the deck, dropped over the rail onto the dock and joined me with a cheerful "Iorana."

"I am Aroa, mate of the *Tiare*—I have some pearls fresh from the lagoon at Penrhyn . . . see?" and he poured a dozen seed pearls from a folded paper into the palm of his hand and extended his cupped palm toward my flashlight. They were mostly tiny, but considering three that were really large for seeds, I agreed to take the lot for $5.00.

The next afternoon I went aboard the *Tiare* and shook hands with the last active schooner captain really to epitomize the South Seas. A couple of hours with Captain Benton in his cabin in the *Tiare* was just about as salty an experience as a man can have in a lifetime.

Born in Glasgow in the '80s, he had been brought by his parents to New Zealand as a baby. He had been at sea since he was ten years old. Cabin boy on the *Richmond,* the *Orion,* the *Sydney.* He also served on the ill-fated bark *Olive Ryno,* skippered by the notorious Boozy Ben who had been commissioned to buy pearls at Penrhyn. Ben took the *Olive Ryno* to San Francisco — jumped ship with the 10,000 Chilean dollars that had been entrusted to him and never was heard of again.

A short man, with a toupee-like white thatch and young, merry eyes that belied his advanced age, Benton loved to talk about the sea and his years upon it. As I leaned back on his bunk under the inverted compass that hung there, my eyes roamed around to rest upon a curious gilt-framed oval mirror that was badly in need of silvering and hung next to a shelf piled with battered toilet articles.

"Ooo, I've got a few things around 'ere that might hinterest yer — that there mirror, what's left of it, came outta the *Seeadler*—it was the bloody Count's own. And 'ere's one for ye," handing me a book titled *Brown Man, White Woman,* published by Hutchinson of London: "hit's a story about this ship. The fellow Richards wot wrote it wasn't aboard the *Tiare* more'n 'arf an hour right 'ere at this dock." I read:

> The *Tiare Taporo* ran into a storm the second day out of Penrhyn. Ominous cloudbanks, lit intermittently by forked lightning, rolled overhead, and thunder roared a warning. We hove to and waited, with no other canvas out but a reefed mainsheet. . . . We let go the reefs in the main sheet, and headed in the direction of the island. . . . But the fates were against us. The wind veered round, a terrific squall struck the ship, and the mainsheet blew in ribbons with a loud report. A huge sea swept the lifeboat overboard and battered in the port side of the main saloon aft. I thought she was not going to rise out of that deluge of solid water. I have a faint recollection of being thrown to the deck, and of lying in the lee scuppers, gasping for breath. The

same cataract carried two sailors overboard. Somewhere out in that boiling smother of whitened foam, a voice called out, the voice of our bos'n. But we could not save him. We were running before the wind under a triple-reefed foresail.

"Some bird, that Richards—I told him ten times that the mainsheet is a *rope*, not a sail. 'The mainsheet blew to ribbons,' 'ee says, ho, ho, ho. And 'ee talks about 'the *reefed* mainsheet,' ho, ho, ho. And that stuff about losin' the bos'n and two sailors overboard. Ho, Ho. This ship ain't ever been in trouble, lost anybody overboard or nothin' like it."

The captain went on to explain that only twice in the ship's history had any slight damage been done. Once the bobstay parted while at sea and two natives fixed it, hanging over the bow in bos'n seats. The other bit of damage was done the trip before this one. The ship was heading home from Penrhyn, with her hold pretty well filled with cargo. She had 55 tons of copra, five tons of shell, 68 pigs, and 122 natives. One morning, just as the early sun was climbing out of the sea, Benton, lying in his bunk, heard a terrific lot of shouting and commotion on deck, and a splintering of light woodwork overhead and forward some-were. He had felt the boat jibe and could see in an instant on his over-head compass that something was wrong. Before he got to the helm the boat had jibed back again. But what a sight met his eyes! The cabin top had been crushed like an eggshell and from its splintered depths a tangle of arms and legs fanned the air, and baskets of fruit and small household goods tumbled forth in great profusion.

The boat had made an accidental jibe and the boom had swung over to wedge itself to a stop in the mass of humanity draped all over the cabin top. To extricate the boom, the boat was immediately jibed back again on its original tack. Fortunately the old cabin house gave way, so instead of crushing a lot of natives the pressure merely pushed them down into the copra hold. Miraculously, no one had been hurt.

Captain Benton had a trick of setting up tots of rum, then lighting a cigarette and letting it dangle from his lower lip until it went out. Before he would get around to lighting up afresh he would talk about a dozen different subjects, intruding one upon the other, as thoughts occurred to him in rapid sequence.

"Here's one for ye," he said, reaching to his shaving shelf for a small teacup whose handle was broken off. "Well, I'll be . . ." he exclaimed, banging the cup upside down on the table. "I 'ad a dozen little pearls in that cup I was gonna give yer for the missus...that damn mate o'mine...I bet he took 'em ashore an' sold 'em to some bloke for a couple of quid. 'E's a wonderful mate, though...I want you to meet Aroa...I never take the *Tiare* to drydock when copper sheathin' is fallin' off 'er.... Aroa can tack on a plate under water faster than most men can do it in a boat yard. 'E's been 17 years on this ship...an old pearl diver. 'E can do anything, 'e can. Speakin' of pearlin', let me tell yer about Suwarrow. There's a bloody island for ye." Benton reached across the chart table to flick a copra bug off my collar. "You and I could lease Suwarrow fer 5 pounds a year from Henderson and MacFarlane of Auckland. That lagoon 'as more pearls in 'er waitin' to be picked up than all the rest er the pearl islands put together. Nobody goes there ...natives say she's haunted...old Bully Hayes massacred a copra gang there in '91.... Even the palms is haunted.... When a boy climbs a tree for nuts, over she comes—full of white ants.... She's haunted, they say...skeletons all over the place. And the sharks, man! No skin divin' in that bloody lagoon. Gotta put machinery in there an' scare the blighters away. Wot a lagoon, man! The *Queen Mary* could go in there an' hankor. Pearl shells is supposed to be wormy, too, they sez, but that's jus' the old ones. Plenty o' new ones, I sez. But lumme, them sharks, man! I might lease 'er myself. Huh—5 pounds! Spend that much in one night in Papeete."

A cockroach as big as a field mouse walked slowly across the cabin floor.

"Now, Victoria, there's an island, man. I gotter down 'ere for Lat. 7° S. and Long. 161° W. Everybody sez she ain't there—er anywhere. She ain't on no chart that I ever seen. But she's on *this* bloomin' chart. I put 'er there meself." Benton moved one of three bottles of rum that were holding down the chart before us and showed me Victoria approximately 1,000 miles due north of Rarotonga. Victoria, he said, was a disappearing island. He had seen it a dozen times in as many years. None of the admiralty books or charts had ever mentioned it, but here it was on the rum-spotted, home-made chart before us.

"Once we was hankored off Wallace near Samoa in the *Southern Cross,* and the men got in a bloody jam from bringin' girls aboard from a convent. Bad business on a French island. The whole stupid lot of 'em was tried aboard the *Calliope* in Samoa an' fined 100 pounds each."

The old man didn't like tax collectors or lepers. He told about how the Parker brothers of Auckland had leased one of the Tongan islands and stocked it with sheep. When the Tongan government tried to impose a tax of one pound per head, old John Parker drove the entire lot of 2,000 sheep over a cliff, burned the buildings, and chucked the enterprise. The French in the Marquesas had put two cows and a bull on each island; covered the area with beef. Then they decided to tax the Marquesan chiefs 40 head each trip, and called for cattle every month until the supply ran out.

Once when Benton, under contract to a Tahiti syndicate, had the *Southern Cross* at anchor in Taiohai Bay in the Marquesas, the French administrator sent a longboat out with instructions that he take two lepers aboard for passage to Papeete. This really brought out the independence of the old man.

"I sent 'em back with a note to the guv'nor that no leper comes aboard this 'ere ship. I got the English flag under me bunk, an' if a leper steps aboard I break 'er out an' me and the crew all gets off."

The old man talked of hurricanes. He had been in three — always ashore at the time. Every horror written about hurricanes had been understatement. Hikueru was the worst one—263 natives were at the atoll pearl diving when it hit. Waves 30 feet high smashed across the entire island and washed most of the palms and the natives into the sea. The natives had been warned to stay low in the trees, but most had climbed to the uppermost fronds only to blow away with the palm tops. After it had abated, a heroic priest supervised activities and had the 26 natives who were still alive dig in the sand on the leeward side for coconuts and canned beef. They found the iron top of a pipe-style bedstead and proceeded to distill sea water in it, as they knew they might have a month to wait for aid to arrive.

He flashed back to "blackbirding" (compulsory labor recruiting) in Melitia and Numea; to "laboring" (volunteer labor recruiting) on the *Sydney Belle;* to taking the old steamer *Timor* through the mission stops of the Solomons, where half a pound of nigger-head or a *pareu* was standard trade goods for enough cordwood to keep the boilers going a week. He spoke of taking loads of guano from Surprise Island. Of a shipwreck, and sailing an open boat from the Chesterfields to St.

Vincent's Bay in 24 days . . . with two gallons of water and half a tin of ship's biscuits.

Present-day routine aboard the *Tiare* was rather prosaic for Captain Benton. The buxom 89-foot boat was slow. Even in a gale he doubted whether she made eight knots. She was too stodgy to come about in the normal way. He always backed the main and wore her around. There was no pretense of ship routine or discipline. Lookouts or watches were unnecessary, because natives could always sense a landfall with radar accuracy. On many a black night, when Benton wasn't too sure where some strong current had carried him, he would be roused by the sharp shout of "aau!" (reef!) from a dozen native throats at the same precise instant. And always with plenty of offing from the danger.

Benton was such an interesting character and such a good story-teller it didn't matter how much he embroidered the truth. For a few hours of really relaxed listening, one would rather be his captive audience than spend five minutes listening to "comment" from any radio or TV personality in the world. As we drained a final spot of rum, Benton referred with great affection to his old friend Captain Winchester, Mrs. Hall's father. The late Joe Winchester had been skipper of the *Tiare Taporo* for three years when she was under the French flag.

"I sez, 'Joe, why in 'ell did ye tell them tourists, what come aboard in Papeete, so many bloody lies?'"

"'John,' 'e sez, 'I 'ad t' tell 'em something!'"

We were fortunate to be in Rarotonga for the festival of the debarkation of the war canoes. On this occasion, dozens of the best dancers of the island doffed their store clothes and dressed in grass skirts to perform in pantomime the rites of the ancient war parties that legend says took off in great double outriggers to sail southwest to conquer the aborigines of New Zealand and establish the virile Maori tribes of that area. This dancing was a lot of fun, and the men who partook of it threw themselves wholeheartedly into the spirit of the occasion. We had seen dancing of some sort on each of the islands we had visited, but we never tired of it, and in many ways it will always be memory number one of the voyage. Much of the dancing in the French islands had been more violent than the pageant of the canoes, and in the latter the emphasis was on derring-do rather than romance. Long lines of warriors paddled in beautiful abandon, chanting the story of the hegira to the distant southwest, while bailers swung polished coconut scoops, and high priests and chiefs swayed to the rhythm of the hardwood tom-toms.

Then one fine afternoon we had a farewell luncheon for Harry and waved him and *Viator* out the pass bound for Samoa, Hawaii, and San Francisco. Harry had engaged as his mate Timi V, an 18-year-old native lad whose main ambition in life was to sail through the Golden Gate and thus see America. For Timi, San Francisco included within its metropolitan area all the states plus New York and Chicago. It was a high island completely surrounded by deep water and of course loaded with skyscrapers, as advertised in Rarotonga movies.

Harry had managed to stock the ship with many things the larder had been shy on for months. Orderly Rarotonga, lush with green vegetables, potatoes, and other English-speaking foods, offered a lot to choose from, and as a final gesture the cook at our boarding house put a chocolate cake aboard, neatly iced "BON VOYAGE." As *Viator's* hull moved toward the sunset, Hazel and I waded into the lagoon shallows to follow with our eyes the last bit of whiteness on the horizon—a triangle of sail above a beloved shipmate and an exquisite craft. After months of close contact with skipper and boat we knew that both would make the passage without difficulty—we knew it just the way one knows those things, not from reason but from faith. A 14-page letter, received by us months later in New York, told how Harry had picked up a second lad in Samoa, made a stop at Hawaii, and was blessed with good weather for the sail back to America. In all, he covered about 10,000 miles in *Viator* in a year of island hopping.

As for our own passage plans, the *Waitapu* was due September 24 from Sydney. It would make one stop at Tahiti and proceed to San Francisco to land us home around October 15. The mail boat, so called, was really a large copra carrier, her entire hull being used to transport the stuff. Passengers were carried as a special favor of the line and the accommodations were anything but spacious. Hazel and I were very lucky to get aboard, however. These Australia-San Francisco mail steamers came through only every two months, and since they carried but eight passengers they were booked solid for months in advance. By virtue of a great deal of cabling to both Sydney and Tahiti and the sudden circumstance that a couple who were going through decided to get off at Rarotonga, we were able to engage two bunks. Hazel roomed with three women in the port passenger cabin and I with three men in the starboard accommodation.

When at last the homeward-bound *Waitapu* was off the pass at Tahiti, it marked for us the completion of the circle we had begun counterclockwise through the islands so many months before. As a small white fishing launch brought the pilot alongside and he climbed up the rope ladder to the rail, we realized that at last our island saga had ended. In a few hours the *Waitapu's* gaping hatches would have swallowed up the prodigious pile of copra stacked at Papeete's quayside, and the vessel would then commence the slow 3,200-mile transit back to civilization.

We spent a couple of hours ashore, revisited the yacht club, and had a round of rainbow cocktails with friends who couldn't believe that we had done our ten islands exactly the way we had set out to do them and were headed home—whole, hale, and hearty. Life around Papeete, they one and all assured us, never changes. The show, staging, and scenery remained constant and the same cast of characters was busy playing out the old parts.

Three yachts from the United States had arrived while we were away. Two were fairly large, and during overhauls were trying to sign up native crews to replace shipmates who preferred island life to further watches at sea. The third, a 36-foot yawl, the *Amigo* from San Pedro, California, had been sailed thither by a pair of movie extras who had taken time out from cowpunching in grade-B westerns, to satisfy a thirst for South Pacific adventuring. The *Amigo* had arrived in an uproar of laughter, because when she came alongside the sea wall the cowboys had warned everybody not to help them tie up.

"We're taking her around the world single-handed," they chorused, "and we want to say we did it all by ourselves."

The acacia-shaded paths along the embarcadero were still peopled by little groups of native girls and boys walking their bicycles and chatting and giggling. A couple of carefully dressed French youths in white linen shorts and pith helmets fished at the jetty. The inevitable bus load of natives, trussed pigs, and copra sacks unloaded nearby, to the throbbing rhythm of a pair of guitars and a ukelele.

As the *Waitapu* pulled away from the dock and slid toward the pass, we took off the leis of *tiare* that friends had placed around our necks and, following the custom, tossed them shoreward to the lagoon surface to say we would return.

It was well past midnight, the *Waitapu* was far at sea, and Tahiti but a cloud formation on the horizon behind us, when we opened a plaited pandanus box that had been put aboard just before we sailed. In it we found two beautifully woven braids of tiny translucent shells, one a man's hatband, the other a woman's belt. They were last loving thoughts from three of our first South Seas friends, our Punaauia land-lady and her nieces, Mvana and Tina.

—As this appalling ocean surrounds the verdant land, so in the soul of man there lies one insular Tahiti, full of peace and joy, but encompassed by all the horrors of the half known life. God help thee! Push not off from that isle, thou canst never return.

Herman Melville

PICTURE LOG

On Tahiti's Point Venus stands the most historic beacon in the South Seas. Here, in 1769, Captain Cook observed the transit of Venus and planted a stone marker with the meridian line cut upon it. Cook anchored the *Endeavor* in nearby Matavai Bay.

Entering Papeete's lagoon from the sea, one looks past trading-schooner spars to sweeping uplands heavy with clouds. The white spire of Notre Dame cathedral is a channel guide used by pilots of incoming ships. Acacia trees, shading the waterfront, all but hide the buildings along the Quai du Commerce.

The three-masted supply ship, *Oiseau Des Iles* lies at Papeete's copra wharf. In the foreground, outrigger canoes are propped above the black volcanic sand.

Here, on the beach at Punaauia, we learned the full meaning of the ancient saying: "The palm grows . . . the coral spreads . . . and only man departs."

Sunlight and shadow patterns the pandanus thatch of our bungalows while a white line of surf cuts across the horizon where lagoon and sea meet upon the reef.

Looking east beyond the ruins of Fort Belleau, the Punaauia Valley winds inland a dozen miles to the approaches of Mt. Orohena, highest peak in French Oceania.

Looking west beyond the thick carpeting of shore palms, high breakers curl into the lagoon. Dense cloud formations move with the trades above Moorea's silhouette.

Burial caves between the high lava ledges hold the remains of Tahiti's dead of the pre-Christian era. Miniature canoes symbolized prowess at sea. On one ledge the whitened skull of a small child reposed.

Timi pauses to ponder some perfect teeth. The priests of olden times sent serv-
ants to the caves to bring down ancestral skulls to witness important ceremonials.

On a day of celebration or fête, everyone wears store clothes. A flower worn over the left ear means "I want a sweetheart"; over the right ear means "I have one." These women are not particularly impressed with the performance of the dancers.

In the South Pacific islands most of the dancing is done by men. The hula originated many centuries ago in Tahiti, and was brought to Hawaii by Tahitian conquerors.

Mr. and Mrs. James Norman Hall watch a sunset from the porch of their bungalow at Arue overlooking Matavai Bay. She was Sarah Winchester, daughter of a famed trading-schooner captain. A carved *Tiki* supports a *tapa* lampshade behind them.

This *vahine* wears an adaptation of the ever popular *pareu* cloth. This material, in fast reds and blues, is an importation from the mills of Manchester, England.

An ancient cannon holds *Viator's* stern line at Papeete's quayside. A permanently level gangplank is possible because Tahiti has almost no rise or fall of tide. Below the trading schooner bowsprits (upper left), Moorea looms faintly on the horizon.

Outward bound, all working sails pulling, *Viator* heads for the pass in the reef.

At sea the assistant navigator never missed a watch at the helm. The blouse of *pareu* cloth was designed and tailored by Lin Fung Chu, the leading couturier of Papeete.

Harry Close was an expert at masthead piloting. Reefs with about three feet of water over them are a light brownish color; those with a fathom, a clear green, deepening to a darker green. When off soundings the water becomes a rich purple blue.

Moorea, our second island, offered the
most wonderfully protected anchorage of
the whole voyage. It was like sailing onto
the still waters of a lovely mountain lake.

Turia of Moorea was the most-traveled belle of the Society Islands. She had been
abroad many times, spoke excellent French and English, yet preferred her home-
made thatch bungalow on the shore of Papetoai Bay to anywhere else in the world.

Turia's house has picture windows opening in every direction yet not a single pane of glass to be cleaned. *Okay*, our outrigger, is drawn up on her white coral sand.

The inside of Turia's house, with its ever-fresh hibiscus blooms and tasteful furnishings, has a decorator's touch. The roof of pandanus is a masterpiece of handicraft.

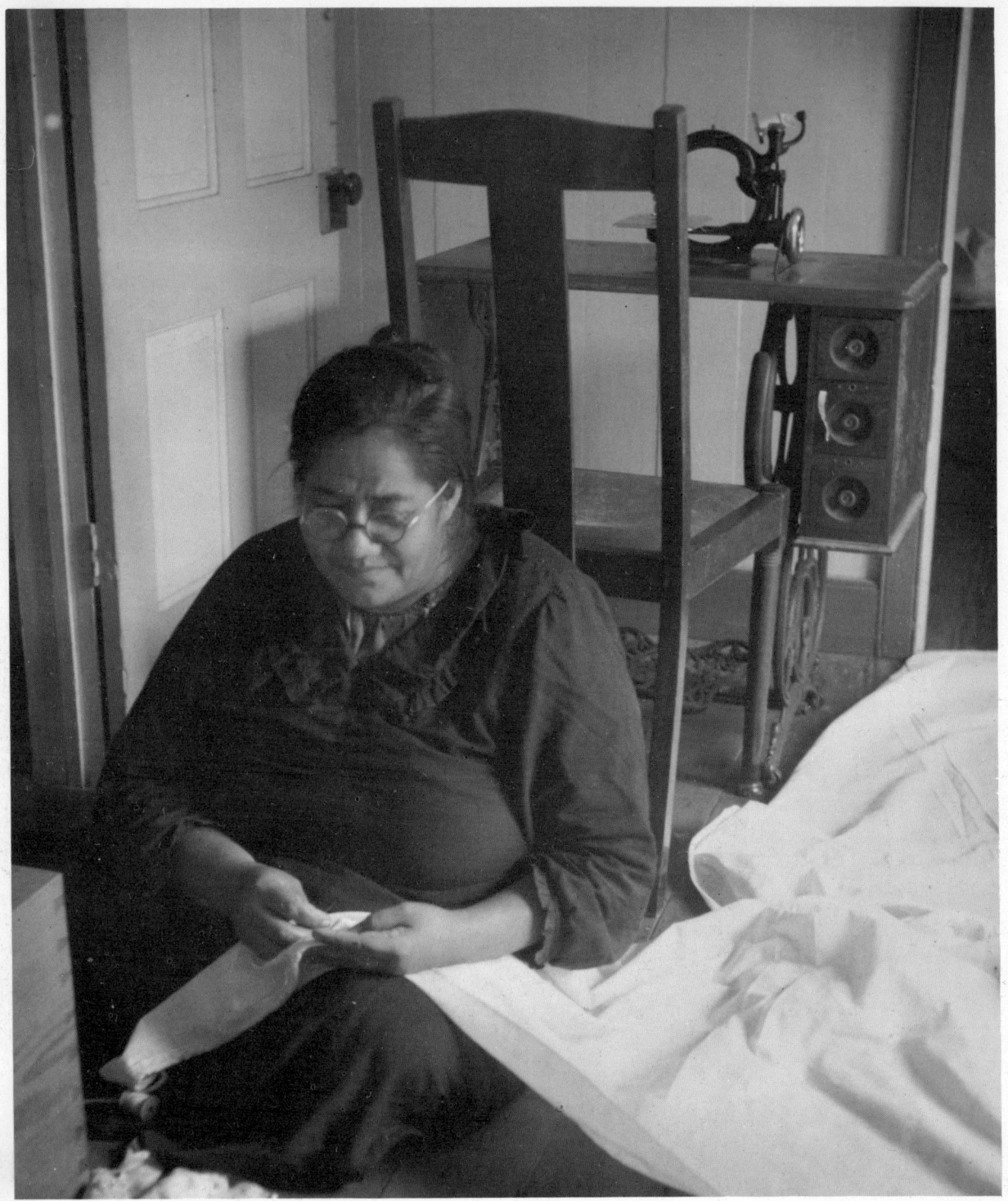

This gentle lady wearing the garb of another era sews *Okay's* mainsail by hand in approved native fashion. On her "Model T" Singer she specializes in dressmaking for a dozen young grandchildren.

Papetoai Bay, the flooded cone of an extinct vol-
cano, has been called the most beautiful anchorage in the world by every skipper who has seen
it, from Captain Cook's day to the present time.

On Huahine, the third island, we found dwellings
on stilts. The thatched village of Moheva sits on
the water near an elaborate arrangement of stone
fish traps. At right is the tin-roofed chief's house.

Moheva's chief, dressed in Sunday best, pauses at the entrance to an ancient *marae*.

The pig has long symbolized island hospitality. This one, after being cleaned and wrapped in leaves, will bake among the hot rocks of a ground oven in ancient style.

A Huahine gondolier poles the taxi dugout which plies the shallow waters between the road's end and Moheva. The gondolier's small son helps with a paddle.

There are scores of swirling streams in the Society Islands, and usually laughing girls to go with them. Three baths a day is an island custom of long practice.

Polynesian grandmothers love to care for grandchildren, and an occasional white child is particularly prized. There are no cleaner people anywhere than these islanders.

The children of Huahine show great ingenuity in making boats. These half-coconut husks with leaf sails move incredibly well in a breeze. Smiles (right), are typical.

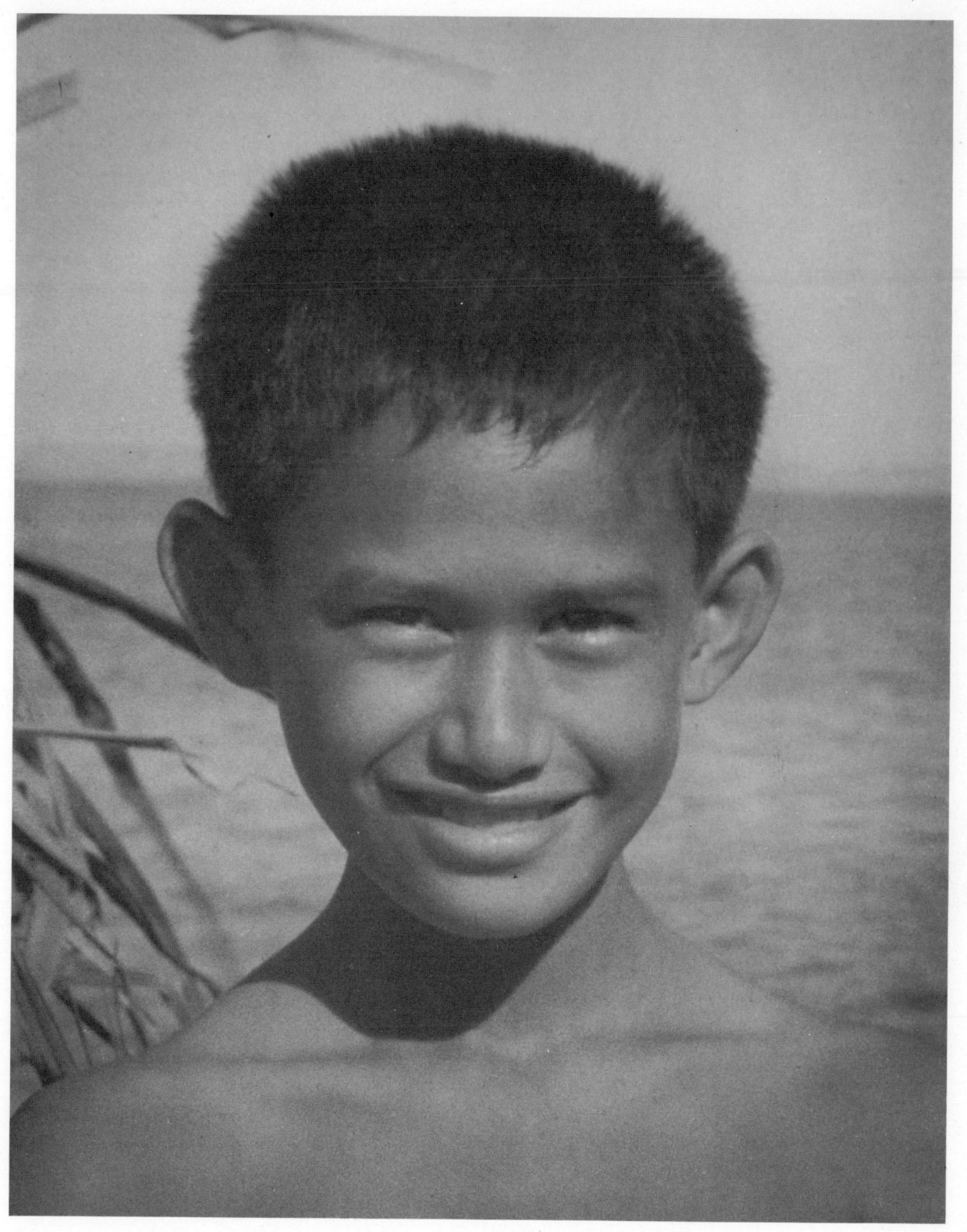

At sea off Huahine, *Viator* is hailed
by a pair of fishermen in a canoe.

As one looks eastward to Huahine from the heights of Raiatea, coral shallows and winding channel are plainly visible between the village of Uturoa and the reef.

A native sits on the outrigger to hold it down while moving at 15 m.p.h.

A family of eight and a sack of copra are a typical load for a large canoe.

The canoes of Raiatea are called the fastest native craft in the world. They have been known to do better than 20 miles per hour on the stretches of the vast lagoon.

Tuemata clenches the handle of the steering paddle and studies the trim of the sail as we start round Raiatea. The paddle blade shows in the clear water below the boat.

The beam of a Raiatea sailing canoe is wide enough for one leg only. On the port tack the paddle is tailed to starboard while the right foot grips the lee rail.

Everywhere in these islands the paraphernalia of fishing is in constant sight. In the midst of drying nets an islander contemplates his live bait trap and canoe.

The children of Raiatea, all excellent swimmers, liked to play around the dock and hang on *Viator's* mooring lines. Some parked sailing canoes are in the background.

Tahaa anchorage brought us the hospitality of Old
William. Here, with stern lines to a coconut tree,
Viator's punt is used to shuttle ashore on Hurepiti Bay.

Old William was at his best when hooking an anchor into coral 15 feet under water.

Teavanui Pass is the only entrance to Bora Bora's great harbor. This picture was taken just inside the reef. The village of Vaitape lies along the shore, at right.

The four hats are an exploring party on Tupua, the small island across the bay from Bora Bora. The abrupt central peaks, eyetooth and molar, are plainly discernible.

Movie posters have no connection with the current billing at the Casino de Bora Bora.

This Bora Bora girl wears a trading schooner comb, a hibiscus flower, and a Mona Lisa smile. She contradicts Darwin's statement that Polynesian women are homely.

La Cloche was the strange outjutting of volcanic rock which rang like a bell when struck.

Marii was the *motoi*, or chief of police, of Bora Bora. He had a British Royal Marine
parade jacket, the gift of a visiting warship, but was too bashful to wear it in public.

A group of the Robeson children sit attentively
while an older sister does an arithmetic problem.

The trading schooner *Denise* was owned by a Chinese syndicate and crewed by Tahitians.

Copra, after it has dried in the sun, is sacked and loaded
into the *Denise's* longboat to be lightered out to the
waiting schooner. Note a sea breaking over the pass.

There is a tense moment when the longboat helmsman
gives the command to start the boat through the reef.

Tubai's swift-running pass in the reef is just barely wide enough for oarsmen to maneuver between coral heads. The helmsman's sweep bends to swing the stern.

In this view from the rigging of the *Denise*, 200-pound copra bags are being loaded.

Tuxedoed movie stars interest these small
fry who divide one wardrobe between them.

A sign in Tahitian explaining all about "The Timber
Queen" hangs outside Bora Bora's large *himine* house.

In the shallows in front of the *himine* house this Bora Bora lad used to stand motionless until just the right fish swam along.

This kindly-faced grandma of Bora Bora wears the black Mother Hubbard which early British missionaries decreed to replace the *tapa* of pre-missionary days.

Emancipated by the French, this young woman of Maupiti dresses as her ancestors did. Her flowered *pareu* ("petticoat") substitutes for the ancient wood-pulp *tapa*.

This young man of Maupiti carries a load of taro root and a basket of papaya. He made a fancy headdress just for the fun of it. Here, play and toil overlap.

From the butte-like ridge that dominates Maupiti one looks west beyond the fringing reef to open ocean.

These graceful canoes are toys four feet
long, made for the children of Maupiti.

Maupitians love to make headgear of hibiscus. This
girl wears a crown as she mixes *poi* in an old bowl.

The bowsprit of the old boat of Fano's father frames the castle-like bluff in this view of our anchorage at Maupiti.

There are no lazy natives on Maupiti. Here a hundred-pound load of breadfruit
is carried down from the highlands as though it were just so many toy balloons.

A small native ketch is drawn up for repairs at Maupiti's dock. This vessel has been sailing in and out of the treacherous pass for years.

Below Maupiti's high rocky peak, lagoon shallows of soft greens and yellows are splotched with darker patterns where purplish coral grows too near the surface.

Roo, the gay head man of Mopelia, stands before his lagoon with *Viator* riding out beyond the shallows. Roo never appeared without some sort of greenery in his hat.

Baby frigates, immovable, and one to a nest, are everywhere on Mopelia's bird islets.

Young frigates patiently await the meals of squid which their parents will hijack for them. When teased, the baby birds are quick to fright and lose their lunches.

The Pacific frigate bird (Fregeta minor) is often called the man-of-war hawk because of its attacks on other sea birds. The frigate does not dive for food but pursues gulls and terns to steal theirs. Rangora caught this one, and let him go.

Exotic flowers grow only on the high islands, so lacking blooms for the hair, or over the ear, the girls of Mopelia atoll made coronets of shredded palm frond.

The youngsters of Mopelia race model outriggers, the only sailing craft they know.

A piece of engine is all that is left of
Luckner's *Seeadler* on the reef at Mopelia.

Tioti of Mopelia brings a hundred pound
poou pataitai in from the outer reef.

This orchestra of Mopelia boys made copra as the spirit moved them, and made music in between. The "bass drum" is a galley remnant of Von Luckner's *Seeadler*.

Braided leaves and ingeniously contrived headdresses transform Mopelia's copra hands into as fine a Bastille Day dance team as might be found in French Oceania.

Once around . . .
a tuck here . . .
a tuck there . . .
well gowned!

Atau, stocky fisherman-in-chief of Mopelia, could spear a basking shark at 50 paces.

Spear fishing is usually done under water but occasionally as a stunt skilled fishermen will stand above the surge of surf at the reef crevices and take a few.

Under water spear fishing is practiced in the lagoon waters of all the islands. The waters are so clear, the fish so close at hand, it looks easy—until you try it.

This tatooed and goggled Rarotongan spear-fisherman was en route to the lagoon when we asked him to stop for a picture. Note the row of ancient stone seats.

On Rarotonga is an ancient stone, marking the spot where early kings were crowned.

When the *Tagua* comes through the pass for a landing at Avarua, native greeters fill the pier's end to seek news of relatives and friends on distant atolls.

This old fellow of Rarotonga plaits green palm fronds to be used as carrying baskets.

Andy Thompson, Brooklyn born skipper of the *Tagua* was a real student of the arts, and good friend of Nordhoff and Hall, who dedicated *Mutiny on The Bounty* to him.

Captain Benton of the *Tiare Taporo* demonstrates fingertip control as he stands before the abrupt skyline of Rarotonga. He navigated with crude homemade charts.

The trading schooner *Tiare Taporo* sits at anchor inside the reef of Rarotonga, when not plying the circuit of the outer islands collecting copra for export.

Sometimes copra is dried in the husk—hung from a pole by bark thongs. Copra has been a leading export since an early missionary shipment carried a $9,000 payload.

The blast of the conch shell is the South Seas' most primitive sound. It calls friends to a fish drive or heralds a pageant like the one pictured on the next pages.

The dance of the war canoes is a rite observed annually on Rarotonga. The ceremony commemorates the 14th century debarkation of fighting fleets southbound.

No matter where the anchorage, on sailing day *Viator*
was always a focal point of interest for island children.

Harry, Timi and *Viator* head for Rarotonga's pass
and wave farewell to friends gathered at Avarua dock.

POSTSCRIPT: For Prospective Visitors

THE best time of year to enjoy the charms of the Society archipelago is during the months of April, May, June, July, and August. This is the wintertime of these islands, and during this period the southeast trades blow strong and constantly. At this time the sun is well to the northward, and the annual temperature is at its most comfortable minimum. It is the time of lightest rainfall and lowest humidity. During these four months no hurricane has ever been known to strike.

Of the other months of the year, December, January, February, and March are the least desirable. These are the "summer months," when rainfall is heavy and the damp heat most uncomfortable. At this time the sun is south again, and although the recorded temperatures do not look appreciably higher on a chart, something takes place which weakens the trade winds and brings about periods of hot, flat calms, followed every now and again by strong blows and every three to five years by an all-out hurricane.

A periodicity chart in the *Pacific Islands Pilot Directions* shows that December and January are the months most liable to bring the terror of hurricane winds to these islands. Another month in which a hurricane is possible but not probable is February. Tahiti is east and south of the cyclonic track and rarely touched by more than the tail of a storm. The last hurricane to damage Papeete was in February, 1906.

Here is a rain and temperature chart for Papeete, Tahiti:

	Jan.	Feb.	Mar.	Apr.	May	June	July.	Aug.	Sept.	Oct.	Nov.	Dec.
Number of days rain	16	16	17	10	10	8	5	6	9	9	13	14
Average inches rainfall	7.2	9.4	10.1	2.7	4.5	2.8	14	1.5	3.0	5.6	8.4	15.7
Average temperatures	81	81	81	81	79	77	76	76	78	79	79	80

Things to Bring

As indicated in chapter one, almost anything imaginable can be bought in Papeete. Chinese tailors can make any item of clothing on short notice and at relatively low prices. When we go again, we shall take plenty of sweaters for the cool nights of the "winter season." We shall also bring an ample supply of thick-rubber-soled sneakers for jumping around on coral and volcanic rock. Daytime wear for the well-dressed man consists of shorts only, the year round. Add to this, halters or blouses for women. The headgear takes care of itself. The one thing the natives do best is to make hats; fine, closely woven ones from leaves of the pandanus tree. The traveler will be presented with more hats than he or she can possibly use. As for gifts for the natives, one finds these generous creatures are sincerely shy about taking anything. Time and again in the outer islands we tried to give them things, only to be met with the polite equivalent of "no thank you." Practically the only request made of us was "more," when we played the phonograph.

That the islanders coveted nothing of our possessions was shown repeatedly when we left the boat for long periods, unwatched and unlocked. We never locked up anything during the entire voyage, and not once did we find our gear disturbed or miss so much as a box of matches. This complete honesty is one thing that must be attributed to the influence of the church, for all through the pre-Christian chronicles of the first voyagers to these islands one finds recordings of squabbles due to light-fingered native visitors aboard ship.

When we go again we shall take one piece of gear that we know will be a sensation everywhere in Oceania. This will be a Polaroid Land camera, with which we can take pictures of the natives as we go along and present them with prints on the spot. All islanders have a passionate desire for pictures of themselves and their relatives, and we shall be prepared to supply portraits numbering into the hundreds.

Photography

Besides the Polaroid Land camera for native portraiture we shall, when we go again, take the same equipment as on this trip. Two Rolleiflex cameras with plenty of Eastman Plus-X Panchromatic film in tropical pack. The best containers for the cameras are large tin paint cans with pressed-lid tops. In still another large paint can it is wise to sprinkle a few tablespoons of calcium chloride in the bottom, and on top of this put two layers of blotting paper. In tins arranged like this, we stored all exposed film with maximum protection against moisture.

There has been endless hokus-pokus written about picture taking, and too much pontification about exposures, openings, filters, lenses, etc. Almost every picture in this book was taken with a standard formula of a 50th-of-a-second exposure, and careful attention to the light meter for lens opening. There were a few time exposures, notably at the burial caves. For shots in motion, the usual shutter speed was 200. No filters, sun shades, trick lenses, or any extra pieces of equipment were used. To repeat, *careful attention must be paid to the light meter*, because one cannot guess anywhere near the brilliance of the tropical sun in the latitudes of these islands. A standard Weston meter was used throughout the voyage, and so important is this item for successful picture results that the wise voyager always carries a spare, against possible loss or damage.

As for film processing, after leaving Tahiti and the Crake photo shop or its equivalent, there are no chances for film development until one reaches Rarotonga. We felt it would be safer to rely on the tightly closed calcium chloride tin containers to protect the exposed film than to try to do any development ourselves en route. One rule we adhered to religiously: never leave a roll of film in the camera more than 24 hours. We were happy to find at the end of the voyage that there was absolutely no spoilage.

Food

Fresh meat is in short supply on all these islands. Chicken and pigs are about the only things to be had, and these are relatively precious. We never tired of the continual menus of sea food, both of the shell and the swimming types, which are everywhere in abundance. As mentioned elsewhere, our diets were consistently supplemented with such things as bird's eggs, breadfruit, feis, taro, manioca, guavas, bananas, papayas, avocados, mangoes, oranges, and limes, plus the ever-present coconut, all picked up from island to island. Canned goods on the yacht supplied corned beef, ham, bacon, and the usual canned things one carries on camping or cruising expeditions. Tinned New Zealand butter, which we purchased in Tahiti, was a highly successful product. It neither turned rancid nor runny when opened, in spite of the fact that we had no refrigeration. We started off from Tahiti with twenty-five pounds of onions and twenty-five pounds of potatoes in open-mesh sacks, and only the potatoes were a problem. When about half used, the rest of the sack flew away in the form of potato flies. The onions, when sliced and mixed with canned beets and soaked in vinegar, we found to be a highly satisfactory sea-going salad. We conserved our water supply by quenching our thirst from drinking nuts which were always aboard, and on occasion Harry and I used the coconut water for shaving and brushing our teeth.

Our diet, despite the abrupt change from what we had always been used to, agreed with us beautifully, and the simple fact of eating hundreds of meals in peaceful surroundings gave us a health we never knew before.

The only delicacy we constantly yearned for was ice cream. There were times when we thought about nothing but ice-cream sodas, talked about nothing but ice-cream sodas and dreamed of eating whole rows of ice-cream sodas one right after another.

Dangers

Besides the dangers from coral cuts, nohus, eels, and octopuses mentioned in the story, there is always the possibility of needing medical attention when far away from home. When we go again we shall not take our appendixes along nor risk the chance of a wisdom tooth kicking up on an out-of-the-way atoll. Either of these things could be serious in such a spot.

Of the dangers at sea, fire is the worst hazard. Tripping and falling overboard at night is about as bad. Next to these comes the possibility of fetching up on a reef at night in heavy weather, in which case it would be next to impossible to swim ashore. No matter in what form any of these troubles overtake one, there is not a chance of getting assistance, because there just isn't any around.

Transportation to Tahiti

It has always been difficult to get to Tahiti, but soon it may be less so. Recently we checked a number of New York travel bureaus and were told the following: (1) An airline, organized to fly passengers from Hawaii to Tahiti, may be in operation by early 1954. (2) Pan American Airways can fly you to Fiji (which is 2,000 miles beyond Tahiti), but are very sketchy about getting you back from there to your destination. (3) A bimonthly air connection from Australia to Tahiti has recently been announced, but no one dares predict how long it will last. (4) Occasional American cargo vessels steam from New York to Sydney, Australia, and make a stop at Tahiti, the trip taking "about" a month. These vessels have accommodations for 12 passengers, men bunking together and women together, and the fare is $525 per person one way. There is a similar cargo line from San Francisco, and on last inquiry it was booked up a year in advance. (5) One can go from Panama to Tahiti, as we did, on a French boat (Messageries Maritimes) that leaves Marseille "about" every two months.

Polynesia Today

One is frequently queried as follows: "Yes, I know there are innumerable quotes by old-timers on the charms of these islands and their people, but what are they like today?" This question was put to Mrs. Irving Johnson recently in the presence of the writer, and she promptly replied that if today Tahiti were as easy of access as Hawaii, all Pacific tourist trade would be diverted to French Oceania. Mr. and Mrs. Johnson, in their globe-circling schooner *Yankee,* have been everywhere, yet they put Tahiti at the top of their list of enchanting world ports of call.

James A. Michener, of *South Pacific* fame, wrote of Tahiti in the year 1951: "A Paradise. The mountains are like no others I have seen. . . . Above all, Tahiti is Polynesian. Without these remarkable people the island would be nothing.

If Tahiti has held its own so well against the inroads of 20th-century "civilized man," one can be sure the outer islands have done as well or better. Some time after we had returned to our commuting existence we received a letter from Mr. J. S. Bennett, manager of the Donald Company store in Rarotonga. It closed with this paragraph:

"I suppose you sometimes think of this lonesome isle in the Pacific. Nothing ever changes, and I believe that if you visit the island again, whatever the year, it will still be the same. Progress is a word that does not apply here."

There are three other questions that are often asked of us:

1. Would you like to go again? Definitely yes.

2. Were you ever bored? No, the time seemed to fly by like magic and we found to our surprise that we didn't once miss newspapers, movies, radios, etc.

3. What about cost of living today? On the outer islands costs are still negligible as already described. In Papeete one can stay at the simple Stuart for $1.50 per day, or two miles out of town one can enjoy the modern comforts of a thatched bungalow at "Les Tropiques" for $6. — $7. — $8. per day. Restaurant meals range from $1.00 to $3.00, drinks in proportion.

4. Would you like to live in these islands permanently? No, and here is why. The more remote and enchanting a place can be, the more one burns with a desire to share it with others. Unless you have the make up of a true hermit you will, after a few months of delicious solitude, want to tell loved ones and friends about what you have seen and what you have done. It is this yearning to come home and talk about it, that makes you do just that.

Vocabulary

There is a saying that as successive waves of people migrated east across the Pacific there was a continuing diminution of the three C's: color, cannibalism, and consonants. Thus, at the height of the Tahitian civilization, cannibalism had almost disappeared, complexions were a light honey color, and the number of consonants in the language had been cut to eight: F, H, M, N, P, R, T, V.

Taken all in all, however, this language with its 13 missing consonants is a pleasant soft thing to hear. James Hall has said that, even before he understood a word of it, he liked to sit on his porch at night and listen to the musical blend of native voices as couples strolled along the Broom Road.

The French do what they can to teach French in the schools, and they use it officially around Papeete, but on every hand the Tahitian language is still the prevailing means of communication. We found this to be true, just as Pierre Loti had found it so when he attended the court of the aging Queen Pomare in 1872.

There she sat on her throne of gilt and red brocade, a large tray of pandanus cigarettes at her right hand, a royal interpreter at her left. The queen spoke French as well as any Parisian but proudly refused to utter a word in other than her native tongue.

Loti was much impressed by the vast number of mystical words in Tahitian. "The sad, weird, mysterious utterances of nature: the scarcely articulate stirrings of fancy.... *Faa-fano;* the departure of the soul at death. *Ao;* happiness, earth, sky, paradise. *Mahoi;* essence or soul of God. *Tape tape;* the line where the sea grows deep. *Tutai;* red clouds on the horizon. *Ari;* depth, emptiness, a wave of the sea. *Po;* night, unknown dark world, Hell." Most of these words live in the language today.

Because we could find no such thing as an English-Tahitian dictionary, we decided to make up a small working vocabulary of our own.

All words end in the vowels a, e, i, o, u, which are pronounced as follows: a — ah; e — eh or $\bar{a}$; i — ee; o — o; u — oo.

Thus,   *faraoa* (bread) — *far ah oh ah*
       pepe (hurt)   — *peh peh*
       tane (man)   — *tah nay*
       api (young) — *ah pee*
       nono (white) — *no no*
       paipu (pipe)   — *pie poo*

Starting on the next page is the vocabulary of some 550 words just as we assembled it in our notebooks. For most of it we are indebted to Roo Fiu who gave unsparingly of his time while we were living on Mopelia.

A

above	*i raro ae i*
across	*maiha*
again	*tapiti*
also	*atoa*
always	*afera*
American	*Marite*
anchor	*tutau*
and	*te*
angry	*riri*
ankle	*fatiraa avae*
apple	*apara*
are	*mea*
as	*mai te*
at	*ite*
automobile	*pereoo uira*

B

baby	*aiu* or *pepe*
bad	*ino*
bad man	*taata ino*
bad spirit	*varua ino*
bait	*marainu*
ball	*popo*
banana	*maia*
bank ($)	*fare moni*
bar	*fare inu*
bay	*e roto*
beard	*huruhuru toa*
beautiful	*nehenehe*
bed	*roi*
beer	*pia*
behind	*na muri*
belt	*hatua*
besides	*ra*
better	*maitai ae*
bicycle	*pereoo taataahi*
binoculars	*hio fenua*
bird	*manu*
black	*ereere*
black man	*taato ereere*
blanket	*paraitete*
blind	*matapô*
blue	*ninamu*

boat	*poti*
bone	*ivi*
book	*buka*
bread	*faraoa*
breadfruit	*uru*
brother	*teina*
burn	*paa paa*
but	*tera ra*
button	*pito pito*
buy	*hoo*
by	*pihaiho*

C

call	*pii*
camera	*neinei hohoa*
canoe	*vaa*
carriage	*pereoo*
cat	*pia fare*
Catholic	*Catorica*
chain	*fifi*
chicken	*moa*
Chief	*Tavana*
children	*tamarii*
chin	*taa*
Chinese	*Tinito*
Christmas	*Mahana fanauraa*
church	*fare pureraa*
cigarette	*avaava*
clean	*ma*
clean (v.)	*horoi*
clever	*atuatu*
clock	*hora*
clouds	*ata*
coconut	*pape ari*
coconut (ripe)	*opaa*
coconut (young)	*nia*
coconut oil	*monoi*
cold	*toe toe*
cold breeze	*hupe*
come to me	*haere mai*
cook	*tutu*
cool	*mahana hau maru*
copy	*oti ino*
crab	*paa paa*
cravat	*taamu arapoa*

crowd	*te pue*
cry	*pia*
crying	*tai*
cut	*tapu*

D

dancing	*ori*
daughter	*te tamahine*
day	*mahana*
deaf	*taria turi*
deep	*hohonu*
dentist	*taote niho*
descendant	*huaai*
devil	*tiaporo*
die	*pohe*
different	*é*
difficult	*ata*
dirty	*repo*
do	*e rave*
doctor	*taote*
dog	*uri*
don't	*e iaha*
door	*opani*
dream	*taototoa*
dress	*aahau*
drink	*inu*
drunk	*taero*
drunkard	*taata taero*
dry	*maro*

E

ears	*taria*
East	*hitiraa o te râ*
Easter	*Tau*
easy	*ohie*
eat	*tamaa*
eggs	*huero*
elbow	*pororima*
electric	*uira*
embrace	*tauahei*
empty	*pau roa*
engine	*machine*
English	*Paratane*
enough	*atira*
envelope	*vihi rata*

exchange	*taui*
excitement	*nane*
eyebrows	*tuemata*
eyes	*mata*

F

face	*hohoa mata*
fall	*topa*
family	*fetii*
far	*ite vahi maoro*
fast	*vitiviti*
fat	*fate*
father	*papa*
fear	*riaria*
feel	*fau*
feet	*avae*
fight	*moto*
finally	*ite hopea*
find	*ite*
fingernails	*maiuu*
finger ring	*topea rima*
fingers	*mani mani*
finish	*ua oti*
fish	*eia*
flashlight	*mori pota*
flesh	*inai*
floor	*tahua*
flour	*faraoa ota*
flower	*tiare*
fly	*rao*
flying	*marere*
fog	*hupe*
food	*maa,* or *kai kai*
for	*na*
fork	*patia*
French	*Farani*
fresh	*haumaru*
friend	*hoa*
front	*mua*

G

gasoline tin	*punu mori*
German	*Purutia*
ghost	*tupaupau*
give	*horoa*

give him	*horoa atu*
give me	*horoa mai*
go	*haere*
go away	*haere atu*
go to hell	*gota hero*
God	*Atua*
good	*maitai*
good-bye	*parahi*
good-morning	*iorana oe*
good spirit	*piru*
governor	*hau*
green	*matie*
gun	*pupuhi*

H

hair	*rouru*
half	*afa*
half caste	*tamarii afa*
hand	*rima*
happy	*oaoa*
harbor	*e roto*
hard	*paari*
hat	*taupoo*
hate	*riri*
he	*ona*
hear	*faro*
heart	*mafatu*
her (also him)	*ona*
here	*ionei*
high	*teitei*
hit	*poara*
horse	*puaahorofenua*
hot	*vea vea*
hour	*hora*
house	*fare*
how far	*ne atia*
humid	*haumi*
hurricane	*toerau*
hurt	*pepe*

I

I	*o vau*
ice	*pape toetoe*
ice cream	*pape toetoe*
idea	*manao*

ignorant	*maamaa*
if	*mai te*
ink	*inita*
innocent	*hara ore*
inside	*iroto*
intelligent	*maramarama*
is	*mea*
island	*motu*
Italian	*Italia*

J

Japanese	*Tapone*
Jesus	*Ietu*
joyous	*oaoa*
judge	*ahua ture*
jump	*ona*
just (fair)	*aau tia*

K

kick	*tue*
kill	*taparahi*
kiss	*apa*
kitchen	*fare tutu*
knee	*turi*
knife	*tipi*
know	*ite*

L

lagoon	*roto*
land	*fenua*
large	*aano*
last night	*inapo*
late	*roroa*
later	*amuri*
laugh	*ata*
leaves	*raoere*
left	*aui*
lemon	*taporo*
less	*iti ae*
letter	*rata*
liar	*taata haavare*
lie (fib)	*haavare*
light (v.)	*tu tui*

lips	*utu*	nose	*ehu*
little	*nainai*	not allowed	*tabu*
long	*roa*	now	*i teienei*
look at it	*a hio*	number	*numera*
look for	*e imi*		
love (v.)	*te here*		
low	*haehaa*		
loyal	*haapao*		

O

		ocean	*moana*
		odor	*haua*
		often	*pinepine*
		oh! (joy,	
		admiration,	*aue!*
		fatigue, etc.)	(pronounced "away")

M

make (v.)	*haamani*	oil	*hinu*
man	*tane*	old	*ruau*
mat	*pene*	olive oil	*hinu oriva*
mattress	*maru roi*	onion	*oniani*
maybe	*e paha*	open	*iriti*
me	*vau*	orange	*anani*
meager	*ivi*	ours	*to manua*
meat	*io*	outside	*i rapae*
medicine	*raau*	over	*iria iho*
milk	*û*		
mine	*tou*		
miser	*horoa ino*		
month	*avaé*		
moon	*avae*		

P

Mormon	*Momoni*	painting	*peni*
morning	*poi poi*	pants	*piripau*
mosquitoes	*nonoō*	paper	*parau*
mother	*mama*	parents	*te mau metua*
mountain	*mona*	pass (n.)	*ava*
movies	*hohoa teata*	pearl	*poe*
mud	*vari*	pen	*tuira*
music	*upa upa*	pencil	*penitara*
		pepper	*pepa*
		perfume	*monoi pipi*
		perhaps	*paha*

N

nearly	*fatata*	person	*taata*
needle	*nira*	perspiration	*hou*
net	*upea*	phonograph	*upa upa taria*
never	*aore roa'tu*	picture	*hohoa*
new	*opi*	pig	*puaa*
news	*parau opi*	pineapple	*painapo*
night	*pô*	pipe	*paipu*
no	*aita*	place (n.)	*oahi*
no good	*aita maitai*	plate	*mereti*
North	*apatoerau*	play cards	*pere api*

plenty	*i roa*	salt	*miti popaa*
pole (the)	*te ooa motoi*	sand	*one*
policeman	*motoi*	satan	*satane (tatane)*
ponderous	*teiaha*	school	*haapiiraa*
post office	*fare rota*	science	*itearaa*
potato	*umara putete*	sea	*miti*
pray	*pureraa*	see	*ite*
priest	*orometua*	several	*raverahi*
prostitute	*vahine taiata*	sew	*nira*
Protestant	*Protetani*	shallow	*papau*
proud	*aito*	shark	*mau*
puny	*rairai*	shell	*pupu*
put	*a tuu*	ship ahoy	*tero!*
		shirt	*ahu oomo*
Q		shoes	*tiaa*
		shoulder	*tapono*
question	*ani*	shush	*turi turi*
quick	*haapeépeé*	sick	*nai*
		sister	*te tuahine*
R		sleep	*tooto*
		smell	*hoi*
radio	*radio*	smells good	*monoi noanoa*
ragged	*ruau* or *tahito*	soap	*pua*
rain	*ua*	soft	*maru*
reach	*roa*	soldier	*faehau*
reap	*ineine*	some	*vetahi*
red	*ute ute*	son	*te tamaiti*
reef	*aau*	song	*himine*
remember	*manao*	soon	*aria*
repair	*hamani*	sour	*haua*
repast	*amu raa*	speak	*parau*
rice	*raiti*	spear	*auri*
ridicule	*hiae*	spectacles	*mata titia*
right	*atau*	spoon	*puni taipu*
ripe	*pe*	stammering	*un*
river	*pape tahe*	stamp	*titiro*
robe	*ahu*	stars	*fetia*
rope	*taura*	steal	*ia*
rude	*ava to*	stone	*afai*
run	*horo*	store	*fare toa*
rule	*ture*	strong	*puai*
rum	*lum*	sugar	*tihota*
		sun	*mahana*
S		surf	*are miti*
		Swede	*Tuete*
sailor	*mataro*	sweet potato	*unara Tahiti*

T

table	*amuraamaa*
tablecloth	*vavau amuraamaa*
taste	*huru*
tea	*ti*
teach	*haapii*
teacher	*orometua*
tears	*roi mata*
teeth	*niho*
telephone	*niuniu parauparau*
tell	*faaite*
thank you	*maruru*
the	*te*
them	*raua*
there it is	*tera*
they	*ratou*
thick	*meumeu*
thing	*tao'a*
this	*teie*
to	*ite*
toes	*mani mani avae*
tomorrow	*ananahi*
toothbrush	*poromu niho*
toothpaste	*hiroi niho*
towel	*tauera*
tree	*tumu raau*
tropics	*te mau rua*
twins	*maehaa*
twisted	*pio*

U

ugly	*hupe hupe*
under	*i raro*
undershirt	*pariaro*
understand	*me fifi roa* (I do not)
up	*inia*
us	*tatou*

V

valley	*peho* or *foa*
vegetables	*maa*
vicious	*peu ine*

victor	*re*
vinegar	*vinita*
violin	*fira*
virgin	*paretenia*
virtuous	*haapao maitai*
voice	*reo*
volcano	*ona auhı*

W

wall	*papai fare*
want	*hinaaro*
washing (clothes)	*pua ahu*
war	*tamai*
watch (n.)	*wati*
water	*pape*
waterfalls	*topa raa pape*
we	*matou*
week	*hepetoma*
West	*toparaa o te ra*
wet	*rari*
what	*ta*
wheel	*hui ra*
when	*afea*
where (is it)?	*te hia roa?*
white	*nono*
why	*no te aha*
win (v.)	*ua re*
wind (v.)	*taviri*
wind (big)	*maraamu*
window	*haamaramarama*
wine	*uaina*
winter	*tau toetoe*
wire	*niu niu*
wish	*hinaaro*
with	*ma te*
within	*ia*
without	*ore*
woman	*vahine*
world	*teau*
wound	*pepe*
wreck	*parari*
writing	*papai*

Y

yam	*e ufi*

year	*matahiti*
yellow	*rearea*
yes	*e*
yesterday	*inanahi*
yet	*aitea*
you	*oe*
young	*api*
your	*to oe*
youth	*apiraa*

Cardinal Numbers

one	*hoe*
two	*piti*
three	*toru*
four	*maha*
five	*pae*
six	*ono*
seven	*hitu*
eight	*vau*
nine	*iva*
ten	*ahuru*
eleven	*ahuru ma hoe*
twelve	*ahuru ma piti*
twenty	*piti ahuru*
thirty	*toru ahuru*
one hundred	*hanere*
two hundred	*piti hanere*
one thousand	*tauatini*
one million	*mirioni*

Days of the Week

Monday	*Monire*
Tuesday	*Mahana piti*
Wednesday	*Mahana toru*
Thursday	*Mahana maha*
Friday	*Mahana pae*
Saturday	*Mahana maá*
Sunday	*Tapati*

Months of the Year

January	*Tenuare*
February	*Fepuare*
March	*Mati*
April	*Eperera*
May	*Me*
June	*Tiunu*
July	*Tiurai*
August	*Atete*
September	*Tetepa*
October	*Atopa*
November	*Novema*
December	*Titema*

INDEX

[250]

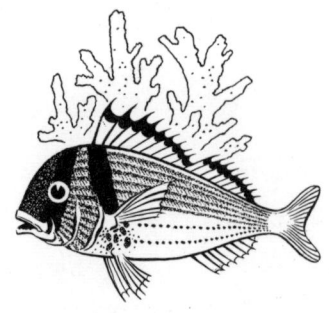

This edition of TAHITI: Voyage Through Paradise *was designed by Robert Blattner and C. O. Wood-bury. The plates and printing were produced by The Case-Hoyt Corporation of Rochester, N. Y. by photo offset. The book was bound by Wm. F. Zahrndt & Son, also of Rochester. The type for the text is 12 point Caledonia leaded 2 points. The Display type is Bernhard Modern. The paper is Wove Hammermill Offset. The pareu pattern used on the binding is authentic and has been printed by the J. F. Auer Company of Mamaroneck, N. Y. Decorations and end papers were created by Robert Blattner. The four-color dust jacket was produced by Everett R. Eaton of The Magazine Engraving Company, Stamford, Conn.*

ᴸOCATED 2300 miles due south of Hawaii — way off any commercial great circle route to anywhere — the Tahitian Islands remain to this day among the most inaccessible of the world's wonders.

There are nine major islands and atolls in the group: Tahiti, Moorea, Huahine, Raiatea, Tahaa, Bora Bora, Tubai, Maupiti and Mopelia. A wise French government has prevented their exploitation and encouraged the retention of Polynesian ways. The tenth island visited by the Egglestons —Rarotonga—is 500 miles to the Southwest and a member of the Cook group, under New Zealand mandate. Below is the 32-foot *Viator* in which the Voyage through Paradise was made.

GEORGE T. EGGLESTON

About the Author

ALTHOUGH he comes from an early New England background, George Eggleston is a native son of California. In 1929 he was graduated from the University, at Berkeley, where he edited the monthly *Pelican*. Arriving in New York he became a contributor to the old *Life* magazine of Charles Dana Gibson. Before he was twenty-five he was the magazine's editor-in-chief. When Henry Luce launched the big weekly *Life* he appointed Eggleston to the first board of editors of that magazine. Since 1945 Eggleston has been one of the editors of *The Reader's Digest*.

From early boyhood Eggleston had a yearning to voyage in the South Seas. He finally did what many have dreamed of but few have ever attempted. He took time out from a busy job to spend the better part of a year in the Tahitian Islands.

In the summertime, when not at the *Digest*, Eggleston is apt to be found on his sloop *Tiare*, cruising between Long Island Sound and Nantucket.

TAHITI

VOYAGE
THROUGH PARADISE

The story of a small boat passage
through the Society Islands

by GEORGE T. EGGLESTON

with 100 photographs by the author

IT TAKES several months to get through
the fascinating islands described in this
picture-log. That is perhaps why so few
books have told of the wonders first chron-
icled by Captain Cook in 1771 and subse-
quently immortalized by Charles Darwin,
Herman Melville, Robert Louis Stevenson,
Paul Gauguin, Jack London and the late
James Norman Hall.

Realizing a life-long ambition, Eggleston, on a leave of absence from business,
decided to see for himself these islands—
each a paradise—which he had read about
in the works of the few lucky individuals
who had preceded him. He and his wife
set out from Tahiti for 1000 miles of island
hopping in a 32-foot schooner, poking in
and out of places that few others have ever
seen.

As James Norman Hall once put it:
"There is a magic about these islands that
is time-defying; that loses nothing of its
power however long continued one's as-
sociation with them may be."

Let the reader experience for himself
this particular magic in the pictures and
text that follow.

N

SOUTHERN CROSS

SOUTH PACIFIC

OCEAN

Rarotonga
21° 14′ S.
159° 46′ W